REAL DIVAS WIN #2

"STORIES OF

FAITH, SACRIFICE & VICTORY"

_____

COMPILED BY

TIFFANY A. GREEN

REAL DIVAS WIN VOLUME #2
@Copyright 2020 by Tiffany A. Green-Hood

All rights reserved. No part of this book maybe reproduced or transmitted in any form or by any means without prior written permission from the author.
ISBN: 978-1-953638-06-9

Printed in the United States of America
This book or parts thereof may not be reproduced in any form, stored in a retrieval system, or transmitted in any form by any means-electronic, mechanical, photocopy, recording, or otherwise-without prior written permission of the publisher, except as provided by United States of America copyright law.

PUBLISHER
TA MEDIA & PRODUCTIONS LLC
DALLAS, TX 75240
www.PUBLISHYOURBOOKTODAY.INFO
WWW.TAMEDIACO.COM

Unless otherwise noted, all Scripture quotations are taken from the Holy Bible, King James Version
(PUBLIC DOMAIN PER BIBLEGATEWAY.COM)

Holy Bible, New International Version®, NIV® Copyright ©1973, 1978, 1984, 2011 by Biblica, Inc.® Used by permission. All rights reserved worldwide.

The Holy Bible, English Standard Version. ESV® Text Edition: 2016. Copyright © 2001 by Crossway Bibles, a publishing ministry of Good News Publishers

Real Divas Win ™ Volume #2

TABLE OF CONTENTS

1. TIFFANY A. GREEN | **7**
2. DEE STEVENS | **16**
3. YVONNE HENDERSON | **25**
4. CARMESHA SMITH | **35**
5. LADONNA MARIE | **45**
6. JACQUELINE CARTER | **53**
7. PAMELA STONE | **61**
8. SHELLY LEE | **66**
9. AYANA MICHE' | **76**
10. LATOYA MOORE | **83**
11. MARCIE WILSON | **94**
12. NICHOLE STOKES SHARP | **109**
13. JILL ALLISON | **123**
14. SHERMIA TAYLOR | **132**
15. YOLANDA IRVING | **143**

Real Divas Win ™ Volume #2

16 SHERRY CAROL BEAN | **150**

17 ALIADA DUNCAN | **160**

18 CHERISE BROWN | **174**

19 LESLIE EPPS | **177**

20 FELECIA BELL | **183**

TIFFANY A. GREEN
THE SEASON OF RELEASE

Tiffanyyyyyyyyyyyyyyyyyyy, was how she called my name when I was outside playing? Well not really playing but most times being the laughingstock of the crowd. This was the introduction to my best friend's low self-esteem and rejection. They've been with me most of my life. Surprisingly those you would think would have protected me from them like family members, used them as weapons to help in destroying the beautiful little girl with the sad face. I grew up never really having friends who were real, but those who just tolerated my presence. This was the norm in my life. Later down the road, I found out my mom experienced this same thing from the same people who should have protected her. Family oftentimes is presented as a supportive team who will be there to protect you and who love you. Lol. Not always the case. Most times they can be worse than a total stranger. These two best friends, rejection and low self-esteem, had an entire plan for my life I never knew existed. I'm sure you've read and heard about horrible situations of prostitution and drug abuse; well, my story didn't come in that realm but another realm from the same root. These two friends often made me feel like I didn't matter, and I didn't want to live. I always felt like I was ugly, and no one wanted me. I was never sure where this came from, but this totally made a fool out of me throughout my days in grammar school and high school. I've never had a conversation with my mom or my dad about these issues, but I don't blame them for anything. When I think back, this would have given them the opportunity to pour into me some love and wisdom that I always knew they had for me but didn't quite know how to give me something they were not shown themselves.

Getting pregnant at 14 was the most embarrassing thing I experienced in my eyes. Now I look back and say, it was a total blessing. I couldn't understand why no one ever reached out to say, it's okay Tiffany, it's going to be okay. My parents took very good care of me during this time, but there was a healing and detox that needed to take place to destroy the two friends that stayed around no matter what. With all the things I could talk about, one thing designated in my head was when I realized just two years ago, I was molested. This may sound crazy but yes, it's real and it really happened. I researched to find out why this just surfaced now and I'm a grown woman. Or why I didn't realize at the time what was going on. It is called a suppressed memory or repressed memory. ... Repressed memories are memories that have been unconsciously blocked due to the memory being associated with a high level of stress or trauma. I do remember I was around 7 or 8 years old at the time. The perpetrator was a female of Mexican descent. She lived a few houses down on the same block I grew up on. She presented the act like a game which involved me performing sexual acts on her. It's crazy because I can remember things, she would tell me to say and do. And I remember walking home from her house feeling awkward, weird and uneasy. People on the outside will say crazy things like, you knew what you were doing. How come you didn't tell anyone? Well truthfully, I don't have any of those answers. I didn't know what was happening and by the time I was 14, I found myself in several situations out of my control. I remember going to a party, ended up in the bathroom having sex with a guy I just met. I was 14, he was 21. People place labels on you like, oh she's just fast and she's into them, boys. Let me explain something to you. I was not into boys like that. Of course, as you grow your, natural instinct is to have a boy in school you like or even church but never was I into having sex. When I did have sex for the first time, in my mind it was nothing to brag about or enjoy. For years I had sex several times and did not enjoy it. What would draw me in most times was the attention of men. This was simply the effects of rejection, but I didn't know this at the time.

I found myself in situations where I knew I would have to have sex. It was like I was numb to emotions or the enjoyment of it. I clearly remember this guy at my dad's car wash calling me and telling me I was going to be his woman. He was cursing and demanding, and again the only thing I heard was attention and that he liked me. Let me tell you, this man was 35 I was 15. He was the cousin of a well-known drug dealer that was frequently at the car wash. All the drug dealers were there faithfully and always flirting. Meanwhile, at school, no one asked me out to the dance, prom or even bowling. So naturally I would gravitate to the attention of grown men. I had no idea this was a trap to destroy me. I ended up hanging out with him one night. I remember lying and telling my dad I was going to a concert. My mom was at a Church retreat that weekend. I remember sitting over my friend's house and paging him and a few other guys I would talk to. He said he was coming to get me. I had no idea what I was in store for on this day, again, I'm only enjoying this so-called attention but this night I was scared... He picked me up drunk and driving. He took me straight to a hotel, actually it was a motel. I knew I was going to have to have sex with him in order to get back home. He was so drunk he fell asleep right after we had sex. I kept trying to wake him up, I knew my dad told me I had to be home by 12. That's all I knew and that all I could think about. I had about 13 dollars in my purse. The sex was very uncomfortable as he was very large and going into my 15-year-old body. I was scared and didn't know what to do. Who would I call, and would they believe me? With God as my witness, I enjoyed not one moment of this. My thoughts now were scared, nervous and praying I did not contract any disease... This was only one of the critical times where God had my life covered with the blood of Jesus. It's odd writing this in 2019. Creating a brand like Real Divas Win is breathtaking. I realize I must be the leader in exposing all the hidden things designed to destroy my life and kill me. Exposure needed to happen in order to preserve my freedom. I refuse to live in bondage and be afraid to speak out about these things. Yeah, they may whisper and point fingers but all I know is it's my time to shine. My transparency is my tool to reach women and help them be set free. My mom was saved for real. She had a serious prayer life I couldn't comprehend at the time what it all meant, but I just knew she was serious about Jesus. Little did I know, it was all a setup. My mom was an intercessor, her tongues were like an Indian language. She was very familiar with the power of God and operated with a strong heart of love and forgiveness. She too had been rejected as a child and an adult, by her parents and siblings. By the time I was 15 I was ditching school on a regular and drinking heavily and sleeping with men I knew nothing about. No one knew. Not even me. By the age of 18, I was responsible for 2 children and no high school diploma. I found myself in an abusive/toxic relationship and I got pregnant 3 more times and had 2 more abortions and one miscarriage. I was not using any birth control or using any protection. So why am I saying all this, because I can still say I'm blessed and called to break generational curses off my bloodline. Through the judgment of people, through living a life where I was totally lost and thought I had no purpose and no direction, God still favored me. There's a scripture that says I will make your name great. My wins come from all the stuff I've been with a long list of several accomplishments I hold close to my heart. Many have no idea of my journey. I'm exposing my story because it's my responsibility to motivate, encourage and uplift. The world is filled with lost souls that want to be restored, renewed and revived. My story is my story, it's not to be hidden or ignored anymore. It's not to impress anyone. Deliverance is a process. I realize to be totally free I must release all this baggage I've been carrying. The men I slept with, the friends I followed that didn't give a damn about me, the names I've been called, the bad relationships because I was rejected and was attracted to rejection, the day I was choked by my daughter's father while

I was 8 months pregnant, there's so much more. Y'all ain't ready for my story. Judgment is for the birds. I remember leaving church and having some Mexican Food with a few ladies I thought were cool to be around. We were sharing things we had been through, but obviously, I must have sad too much. The lady who was married, was very standoffish when I asked about her husband's roofing business. I was gifted a whole house for free and it needed a roof. She kept brushing me off telling me he was just a handyman, not a roofer when he had just given someone else an estimate for their roof. And the Holy Spirit showed me, remember the conversation, she doesn't want you around her husband because of what you shared. Well damn, I thought wow. people do this phony stuff in church. Even still I refuse to hide my story, its purpose is to save lives.

MY WINS

Professional wedding photographer for 14 years
I am an Author, Publisher, and Graphic Designer
TA MEDIA & PRODUCTIONS
I received my GED in 2000
I attended Purdue University Calumet
I published and consulted several authors in publishing their books and building their brands.

I have 2 grown children and 4 grandchildren.

2 Magazine Blogs

REAL DIVAS WIN ANTHOLOGY OF THE YEAR NOMINATION WITH IALA AWARDS

The Beautiful Boss MAGAZINE BLOG +

2 podcasts

Connect on Facebook @thetiffanyagreen

flow.page/iamtiffanyagreen

DEE STEVENS

Release. Work. Receive

I filed for divorce on a Monday. It was final on Friday.
I walked away from EVERYTHING when I divorced. I gave up the house and equity that I was entitled to in order to " free up my life". I was in a marriage that was.... just ok. It wasn't "horrible" ... but it was not fulfilling. My husband at the time was very complacent. We did well financially and had huge potential to accomplish amazing things. However, when I would present ideas, dreams, goals or plans to him, he would respond less than enthused or outright turn my suggestions down. He was perfectly fine with going to work 9-5, church on Sunday and repeat. I could no longer live this way. I had been married for 8 years. I had grown too comfortable. I was so comfortable; it had gotten UN- comfortable. I had forgotten who I really was just for a moment as I attempted to become "one" with my husband. That's what wives are supposed to do, right?

You see, I've had a job since I was 14 years old and as early as 24 years old, a single mother I owned 11 income properties and a single-family home for my daughter and I. It all started with an income tax return. I wanted my return to make a difference this time. I decided that I wanted to buy a "building". I knew nothing about real estate and had poor credit but "buying a building" is something I would always hear my mother fantasize about. It sounded like the smart thing to do. I knew because my credit was not strong, I would need a strong down payment. Though I was young, I craved the desire to go out on weekends or buy up the mall. Instead, I made a point to not only save my income tax return, but I saved every bonus at work, every refund or rebate from every purchase. I ultimately saved $20,000 in one year. I figured with $20,000 down at that time, who would say no? Well, guess what? I came across a 2-unit building that cost $50,000. It wasn't the prettiest, but it was move-in ready. I had $20,000 down of the $50,000 and they said yes! Not only did they say yes but a year later, through creative financing and in retrospect probably predatory lending, I was given a bundle which allowed me to obtain ten mortgages at one time! Ten! So here I am at 25 years old shopping around town picking and choosing the properties I wanted and closing these huge real estate transactions. I still worked my full-time job and managed these properties. Soon after my mother fell ill. I sold everything and relocated to be near her as I did not want to manage the properties long distance. Technology and travel were different then. What an amazing ride that was. I did that and it was effortless. I knew I had it in me and could always go back to it.

So now I am married and in my late 30's. I have this savvy real estate mogul inside of me. I wanted to revisit what was dying to be let free... the true me. I wanted to share this with my husband, my life partner. He was not moved by the idea of it. Was it fair that I could never do this (among other things) because I was married to someone who had no goals? That did not seem fair. So, I left. I left and I signed everything over because I did not want to fight over the house and the accounts. I did not want multiple court dates and to be held up from starting my new life. I had a plane to catch.

Within one month of arriving in my new home state of Arizona, I purchased an investment property back home in Chicago. It's a 2-unit building with a 2-bedroom apartment on the first floor and 3 bedrooms on the 2nd floor. It was in foreclosure and I got it for a whopping $15,000! Because I paid cash, I would have no mortgage and the cash flow potential would be upwards of $2000 a month! I rehabbed it and rented it out.

This was an amazing opportunity. It was an amazing opportunity, especially because, by the time I closed, I had just divorced a month prior and left EVERYTHING behind. I stepped out on faith. I quit deeded my marital home and all of its equity to my ex, left all home furnishings, accepted a promotion and moved to the sunny state of Arizona to experience the joys of resort living.

Now there is a lot I could say about this blessing. Blessing is an understatement. I acquired property that could not only provide me with shelter and plenty of equity of my own, but it would also generate income! Though I was always self-sufficient, after being married so long, the thought of being responsible for my own rent payment was frightening. But I still let go of all the material things that individuals usually fight over during divorce. I let go of what was "comfortable" because in actuality I was not comfortable. Within weeks I have a bigger blessing.

I'd be remiss if I did not mention the fact that I had a friend that ultimately became a " strategic partner" of sorts. Though I had a small savings and general real estate knowledge from my previous lifetime, he had the skill and muscle to do the rehab work. After I closed on this property, we shared a celebratory breakfast. As we sat across the table catching up on my recent divorce, congratulatory wishes, and rehab plans, he posed the question to me that would forever change my life.

My partner asked: " What would it take for you to move BACK to Chicago?"

Now to put this in perspective I had JUST left Chicago a month ago. I had JUST accepted a promotion after relocating, settling into southwestern living in my luxury townhome in my gated community. Developing my new lifestyle had taken months of interviewing and networking. My salary was now higher than it has ever been before. So, when my partner asked: " What would it take for you to move BACK to Chicago?", my first thought was that I do not want to do this again. I do not want to interview or network in HOPES of securing employment...ever again. I had flashbacks of commuting back and forth on the commuter train, paying for parking daily or monthly, HOPING for an internal job posting that I would qualify for and HOPE I land the job so that I could move back if that's what I chose to do.

A lightbulb went off at that moment.

I replied: "If I move back, I don't want to have to " work" again."
I had just scored my position in Phoenix. The application process involved flying out to Arizona, multiple virtual interviews and a writing sample. I simply could not see myself tap dancing, wishing and hoping that I would be good enough to be chosen for another position if I were to move back to Chicago. OH, and that's assuming there would be an available position that I would qualify for and more importantly interested me.

Over the next year, I underwent stretches of working over 20 hours a week overtime at my job to build my savings, managing my credit score, and flying back and forth to Chicago just about monthly to assess opportunities and acquire additional property. I maintained a laser focus mindset regarding my transition into full-time entrepreneurship as an author, blogger, realtor, and real estate investor within just eighteen months.

I had given up, signed over and relinquished all of my material possessions to move forward. I let go of a dead-end relationship and was given a new life.

I won't take away from the hard work and partnership that contributed to my success, but I simply cannot miss the opportunity to share an important component of my process. Please know there were many times that I felt that my dreams were too big. There were many times I would sit alone in that Phoenix townhome and there would be a voice asking " what are you doing ?" or " do you really think you can buy up all these properties and walk away from your job?" That same voice would tell me that it's safer to keep my 9-5. That same voice would try to fool me into believing that I did not deserve the lifestyle I was trying to build. So, I began to write out my goals. I would number each goal and write them out 5 times each; pen and paper. I kept a tablet at my desk at work and I would do that for myself every morning before starting "their" workday. Before I knew it, I was checking off those goals and having to write new ones. I was systematically writing a blueprint for my dream life. After a while, I created a playlist of positive affirmations that I would listen to before bed many nights. These affirmations would affirm the fact that I did, in fact, deserve all of my current and future successes. These affirmations would affirm that I had everything I needed inside of me to accomplished all of the things that I dreamed about. These affirmations changed my way of thinking and ultimately my life.

I have the highest hope that the takeaway from what I have shared is that with just a little bit of faith followed but a lot of action, removal of distractions, addition of positive thought, your biggest aspirations will fall right into your lap.

YVONNE HENDERSON
Preyed vs Prayed

Down through the years, I have found myself in situations where I was being preyed on and not prayed for. I would love to say this only happened in the world, but it was in the House of the Lord where I had most of my experiences with this. As a young woman and convert I thought everyone in the House of the Lord was on the up and up. There were three of us, we made a pack and vow to remain virgins until we were married, at least that's what we were being told in Bible Study and on Sunday mornings. Well, two out of three isn't bad. Yes, I watched them get married to men they met in the church, have kids only to have them walk out on them for someone else, or just because they didn't want to be married anymore.

I told God I didn't want to be like that. Well, I met a military man, who reminded me of my dad, you know they say girls marry guys who remind them of their fathers. He was also a minister, so I thought, "okay, this should be alright." Wrong!!! Once he started asking me for sexual favors, I got uncomfortable. He asked me to marry him because I said I was saving myself for marriage. He continued to pressure me saying, "We're getting married so we can go ahead and do it." My spirit said no, once again. That is not what God's Word said. "How can you be asking me to do these things when you should be teaching and living the Word of God as a minister?" He replied, "I have needs and if you won't someone else will." I refused and he moved backed to Atlanta. After being gone for a few months, following his honorable discharge from the military, he had a stroke. He was upset with me because I was not there and began to tell me of another who had been taking care of him. I made a point to visit him after he got out of the hospital, on February 14, 1987, the day we were to be married, to call it off and return his ring. Trusting God and staying on the road less traveled was a challenge. This I believe is where my mindset began to change about the way things were to be.

As a single woman, I made it a habit to go to church, when at home or away. I traveled to Chicago to visit family and of course I went to church. I went to choir rehearsal with them and met the minister of music, who was also a preacher. After returning home I was contacted by a family member who said the minister of music was interested in getting to know and wanted to know if they could give him my phone number. I was flattered and said yes. I said, "Okay, another man of God, this should work, he's more mature than the last one.

We had several late-night conversations and began to develop feelings, so he decided to send for me. I went to visit, and we had a lovely time. He took me out to eat then back to his place to watch T.V., I know you are thinking that was a bad move, but it was nice. He held me, we cuddled. When it was time to go, he dropped me off, kissed me on the forehead and gave me a hug. I thought, "This is how a relationship should be." The next time he had me come down his boys were there. He had me hide in the back when their mom came to pick them up, I was tripping because I just thought he didn't want any drama, which was cool with me.

Some months passed and it happened, he asked me about sex. I told him I was waiting until I was married to do that. He seemed to be okay with it at the time. I'm 22 years old and I'm still holding on to not having sex until I'm married. A few more months go by, we're kissing and hugging then it happens, he goes down, the first time I have ever had a sexual encounter and it was oral sex. He comes up after fingering me with this thin layer of skin on his fingers. This is your virginity, so there really isn't anything left for you to hold on too. I'm feeling good and confused at the same time, but I tell him, "I'm still not ready to have sexual intercourse." He says, "Okay."

The next time I went down the manipulation started. I remember the way he made me feel, but I still did not want to have intercourse, so he sent me back home. Like a junky, I tried to reenact how he made me feel, this was the first time I masturbated and pleasured myself. He stopped answering my calls. So, I told him "Yes." We had intercourse and I felt bad, I didn't like it and it hurt. He said he loved me, and he was going to marry me. Another man of the cloth, I believed would do right by me. We began to work together as a couple. We started spending more and more time together. Then he came up for a Pastor's position. I helped him prepare, I prayed with him, and for him, but when he got word that he had been appointed I wasn't a part of the celebration. He invited me, but I had to sit in the back of the church like a nobody. After service was over on his way down to the Fellowship Hall, he introduced me to his mother as his friend, "his friend" are you kidding me. I went downstairs for dinner and sat among strangers. The ride home was awkward. I asked, "Why he told his mom I was just a friend and not his fiancée?" He said, and I quote "The time wasn't right." "The time wasn't right? Was the time right when you were fucking me last night? Was the time right when you fucked me this morning before church? What do you mean the time wasn't right, we're a couple?" "Things are changing now they think I'm single and I don't think you are First Lady material!" "I was First Lady material before you preyed on me? 1989.

    I go to college damaged, betrayed, wounded, bitter, battered, misled and dejected. I try to stay to myself because

I don't want to be hurt, but I wanted to hurt. So many times, as women we hide inward and mask the truth that lies on the inside. Because of my characteristics, I was displaying, I was known around campus as "The BITCH." I thought this would keep people away from me, but I was more vulnerable than ever. I slept with multiple guys to try and ease the pain I was feeling. I didn't want a relationship I just wanted to feel good (sex). Once we were done, I was done, don't call me, I'll call you was my motto. I never slept with the same guy more than once, if I could help, because that meant attachment and I wasn't trying to get attached. I was selective, but I was still self-destructive. I never used protection because I didn't care about myself. Even in my stupidity, God showed me His grace and mercy. I got pregnant once in my tubs, which resulted in a miscarriage, and I've never had an abortion. I did contract two Venereal Diseases during my stupidity days, but God was right there to carry me through, even when I could not see my way. 1990.

    Third year of college I found a little Baptist Church. The preacher was great, and the choir was pretty good. I go a few times and then I join. The Minister of Music was a music major like me. We hit it off well and became the best of friends. After a few months the pastor asked me if I could type, I said yes, he said he needed someone to type his sermons and he would pay me. As a college student, it was easy money for me. I then became his secretary and he asked me to come up to the church to straighten out his files. I'm thinking everything is good, then it happens. He kisses me, I don't think anything is wrong because I thought he was single. That kiss leads to us making out in his office. Again, I'm thinking, "This is a man of God, he shouldn't be doing this." Then he asks me to help organize his outings and go with him to sing before he preaches. One night it was late, he suggested I stay with him in the hotel and leave in the morning, I agree, you guessed it, we had sex that night. This was different, I was in love. A few Sundays go by and his wife and kids come to church. When he introduces me, I'm floored because I didn't know. I tell him I can't be a part of this, and he tells me, "don't worry, she doesn't care, I do this all the time.

My God, is this a trend among preachers? He asked me to meet him for lunch, I get there, and the table is full of other ministers from around the area. I thought he would be discrete, but he introduces me to them as his special gal, everyone smiles and makes comments like, "You got you a fiery one there." "When you done send her my way." I am embarrassed and uncomfortable. 1993.

After this got married, I thought it was all over. What I found was I was so used to being mistreated it was a part of me. I found myself not feeling worthy of love and that was how he began to treat me. I found myself starting arguments just to have makeup sex all a part of the hurt that I had not dealt with. I began to see the signs of manipulation and self-hatred creep up into our marriage. I started to believe the negative things he would say to me, "ain't nobody else gonna want you!" "You got ugly feet, don't wear sandals because don't nobody want to see that." "Do something with your hair." I began to believe I was not worthy. He accused me of cheating to cover up the fact that he was. He made me feel like I didn't know how to be a good wife and I began to believe it. It was so bad he had his mistress to drop his son off at our house when he was at work instead of asking me to pick him up. I was fed up, I didn't want to live like this anymore, so I decided I was going to punish him in a good way. I sat in our bedroom and waited for him to come in. I heard the garage open then close. I heard the back door open and close; it was time, I want to make him feel as much pain as I did. I positioned myself with the 9mm in hand and pulled the trigger……2001

Well, you know the story didn't end there because I am writing this now. After that incident, I found out I was four weeks pregnant. God spared my life because of the life of my son. I still had to deal with some predators, but I learned how to pray, I developed a relationship with my Heavenly Father that would surpass any relationship. He showed me what love was, and how to love with unconditional.

Seven steps to healing:

1. Pray and ask God to forgive you for your wrongdoings.
2. Pray and ask God to forgive those who wronged you.
3. Pray that God gives you a clean heart and renewed spirit.
4. Pray for God to guide your footsteps into the places He wants you to go.
5. Pray that God will deliver you from those who had you bound.
6. Pray for a better understanding of His word.
7. Pray that God will give you the wisdom and grace to move forward.

These steps have helped me to regain who I am in Christ. Redefine my goals and to move on with dignity. I am not who I use to be, and I am getting stronger and better every day. With these seven steps God has allowed me to make amend with those who were willing and to still pray for those who no longer talk to me. We spend too much time worrying about people who are not worried about us. As soon as I stopped worrying, that's when God started working, I let go and let God have His way in my life. I know have a not for profit organization "Love Lifted Me" Gospel Arts Workshop, where I train and teach people how to use praise and worship to take their life to the next level. Then I have my for-profit design businesses "D.I.V.A. Designs, LLC, which is now located and based out of B & J. Cleaners 2430 South Main Street, Stafford, Texas.

Website: www.divaministries.org
Email: divamimeministry@gmail.com

CARMESHA SMITH
Learning to Win, Survive & Inspire

Both violence and abuse are sensitive subjects. I know this to be true, because it is my truth. I became a victim of violence and abuse both at an early age and in my teenage years. Violence is no longer a silent act; it is now something that has become a part of our lives through the daily news and social media. Violence is defined as a behavior that involves physical force intended to hurt, damage, or kill someone or something. Abuse is another subject that people do not always acknowledge because it can be embarrassing for many people to admit they have been verbally, physically, emotionally, psychologically, or even spiritually abused. Abuse is defined as the misuse, mishandling, or ill-treatment of someone or something. We as humans tend to not want to discuss or display what we have been through, often because we are too afraid to be judged or blamed for someone else's actions. I agree that it can be difficult to share our stories of violence or abuse, but if we do not share our stories, these cycles will never be broken. What many also fail to realize is that by sharing stories of violence, abuse, and most importantly, healing and thriving afterward, their stories will not be able to help others break the cycles of violence and abuse they are living.

I became pregnant with my first child while dating an abusive high school jock. No one knew I was being abused, and I honestly can't recall the first time I was abused or the reason for it. I can, however, still recall all the different times that it happened. How do you make it through when you become a mother at a young age and the father is violent the whole pregnancy? My solutions were simple: keep a smile on my face, keep my emotions in check, and figure out how to adapt, rise to the challenge, and win in each abusive encounter.

During my freshman year of high school, I can remember desperately wanting to date because that is what you do in high school. My parents were okay with me dating at this age. I was 16 years old, I thought I found the love of my life in high school. Everyone was booed up. In the hallways, the lunchroom, by the lockers and in study hall, that's all I saw. I envied them and wanted to be like them. I didn't want to have someone just to have someone; I was willing to wait for someone who loved me and was willing to put that love on full display for everyone to see. I waited, and then I thought I found him. He appeared to be the ideal boyfriend, or so I thought - tall, dark, and athletic. I waited and ran from him for a while, because this was my first and all my girlfriends had boyfriends. I also knew my parents were not going to agree to it, so I waited and snuck around for a while. In time, our relationship blossomed, but there were a lot of bumps along the way. Cheating, abuse, lies and disappointments. I kept at it, thinking to myself, this is love, and things will get better before they get worse. I continued my boyfriend and girlfriend relationship with him in the same manner, still not informing or involving my parents. At that age, I did not know my worth. I thought this was love with a capital L and that my friends were experiencing the same problems. I saw them argue and heard the rumors of fights and infidelity. Because these relationships were with athletes, and we were cheerleaders and all honor students, it seemed that we were all hiding lies, abuse, and personal problems from each other and from those who should have known. No one shared their problems, so we didn't see any signs of abuse.

After my best friend witnessed me being abused once, she was livid with him and upset with me that I allowed this type of treatment and disrespect. She had heard but had never seen (so never had to confront) me about the abuse I was experiencing. I will never forget the day it happened. This started off as a beautiful Saturday morning. I decided my kids and I would go shopping with my girlfriend and her kids. We shopped and took the kids for pizza. We were gone for most of the day, and we had a fabulous time until I arrived home. I never thought me being gone all day with his car would have been an issue, but it was for him. He was standing on the porch waiting for me to return. Back then we didn't have cell phones. only beepers. But, in his mind, I should have been at home. He immediately slapped me so hard that I blacked out. My face swelled up almost immediately. When I came to, I was dizzy and disoriented. This was it. The first time both my young children and my best friend witnessed his horribly violent behavior. I had to make a decision because I didn't want to risk my children being affected and my best friend not being my friend. I realized at that moment that I had to leave.

Days later, I was at my grandmother's house, kids and all. Of course, we continued to play around because I was still confused about his love and abuse. I was caught in the ebb and flow of love and violence that so many women experience. This went on for a short period of time until my family threatened to call the police on him or put me out. I was embarrassed, humiliated, and unbelievably, still "in love" with my children's father. I had to let go!

I took this time to teach me to love me, recognize my self-worth, and get my confidence back. Boy, I didn't realize that LOVE was so painful and so complicated! I learned that I had allowed my self-worth to be devoured by a man for whom I had birthed children. I learned that I can never again love the man who had hurt, embarrassed, humiliated, disrespected, and eventually turned his back on his children and on me. I also learned that I can never let anyone harm me in this way again. I had endured so much during that time. I was learning to heal, live, learn, and grow. My advice to you, readers, is to rise above what you have been told and what you went through. If you survived and you are still unclear about your purpose, learn your worth. According to 1 Peter 3:3-4, "Your beauty should not come from outward adornment, such as elaborate hairstyles and the wearing of gold jewelry or fine clothes. Rather, it should be that of your inner self, the unfailing beauty of a gentle and quiet spirit, which is great worth in God's sight."

Too many of us allow men to define our self-worth. They instead should accept our hearts and see what we can offer. God tells us we are great in His sight. We need to learn to read our Bibles and live how we are supposed to live according to his wishes. One of my greatest disappointments is that I did not have this knowledge and understanding then, back when I was going through the hell I went through. The Bible verses I have quoted are what healed my heart, strengthen me daily, and continue to help me forgive those who have trespassed against me. I what God had for me.

Proverbs 31:25 states, "She is clothed with strength and dignity, she can laugh at the days to come." I have come to realize that I was stronger than how I lived, loved, and was accepted. My dignity was compromised because of the abuse that lasted for years. I stayed; I left; I went back, I creeped, and then I finally left when I was given an ultimatum. Never, ever allow anyone to compromise your dignity, self-worth and your ability to be you! God tells us in Sol. 4:7 that we are "...clothed with dignity and strength." That means you, too!

You are altogether beautiful, my darling; there is no flaw in you. I thought I was flawed because I allowed the abuse to continue for so many years. God created us to be beautiful and know we are perfect in ways that only he knows.

During this time, I sacrificed three important aspects of my life: properly raising my daughters and being a good example to them, loving myself, and learning what God wanted me to know. Today, my daughters are working on their relationship with their father. I felt it was best that we stayed away for a few years until I was strong and independent. I also needed the time to learn to defend myself and to show him he had no control over me anymore. Yeah, he attempted to call or come by my relatives' homes so his family can see the kids; however, he could not be the one to come get them. In order to move on, I needed to sacrifice some things that impeded my forward progress and got in the way of my healing - things that made me revert, people who made me revert. I had to let go, and you MUST let go so that you can get yourself together! I used this time for picking up my feelings, healing my wounds, and looking forward to a brighter future. We aspire to be loved and have love in our relationships. We strive to give and gain love. Love is defined in Corinthians 13:4-7 in four different ways: Storage: Empathy Bond, Philla: Friend Bond, Eros: Erotic Bond & Agape: Unconditionally "God" Love. I positively shifted my life when I learned my purpose and learned to start loving me. I put my children's needs above anyone else's. I took time for myself. I couldn't be good for anyone until I began to release the past and learn to forgive. because if I didn't, I would not have been able to move forward. I shifted my life when God spoke to me with affirmations of His love, my strength, and my dignity. This is when I started to win. Winning comes from forgiving the people who hurt you. Winning comes when you look at your circumstances and say what was I thinking? Winning comes when you look at what you have learned and see the growth you have experienced and the progress you have made. Winning also means you can see the people who hurt you and not get bothered or angry. Winning comes from within; you have to claim your past hurts, release them, and most importantly, forgive. As I look back over that part of my life, I still walked away with some believing that I was a winner and that this was stumbling block. I also believed that these horrible experiences were not going to break me; instead, they were strengthening me for a greater purpose. That purpose is to share with other women that our situations don't define us nor discredit us; instead; it validates our strengths, weaknesses and past. Ladies - we can overcome anything we put our mind to it. We can turn our situations into powerful lessons to share with other women.

Be Inspired! You will be inspired when you know everyone has a past, disappointments, and a story to share. Learning to be transparent not only helps you, but it also greatly helps others. Be inspired when you know you are in control. We have to always remember God is ultimately in charge of our destinies, and we have to learn to live lives that are pleasing to him. You can do whatever you put your mind to - I promise! We have to learn to empower, embrace, and educate each other about surviving abusive and violent trials and tribulations, just like I did. I learned what 1 Peter 5:10 states: "And the God of all grace, who called you to his eternal glory in Christ, after you have suffered a little while, will himself restore you and make you strong, firm, and steadfast." We can be strong. We can be firm. We can be steadfast. We can fulfill these truths with trust in God and fellowship with each other.

LADONNA MARIE
How I Made It Through

As I begin to think about my life and how I made it through. I had to change my mindset and believe in my true purpose. I felt like no one truly got me or understood where I was coming from. I felt lost, in a sense that caused me to turn inward. However, from the beginning, God kept telling me that I was validated and that he loved me and I was like I hear you but not really feel it. Therefore, I continued to look outward at other people to feel the void of what God was trying to do internally. God was trying to show me my worth, and I was still trying to find that physical touch and connection.

However, that didn't work for me, the more I poured out and tried to help others the more I felt rejected. I felt like all I wanted to do was help and others were not grasping where I was coming from. In my soul, God had deposited a need for me to nurture, care for, and encourage others. He was showing me all that was possible with trusting him. He was pouring out his unconditional love to me and I still wasn't getting it. So, after constantly bumping my head up against the wall and trying to get others to understand, I attempted suicide. I felt like it would be better without me here since no one really showed they cared anyway.

I heard the words, you would never be enough, and it almost seemed like they stayed stuck in my head. Writing help me to find a way to creatively express how and what I felt. I'm not sure if I was reading the bible much back then, but from my encounter with God, gave me enough strength to fight through. Over the years it was a series of bad things, negative relationships, feeling hurt, lonely, etc.

Then God said to me that he had plans for me and that this was not the end. He has just rescued me from my brokenness. He made death behave, in order to show his love for me, and I was grateful. I made up in my mind that no matter how hard things got, God said he would over leave me or forsake, and I would be fine. I decided that I wanted to live and I choose life. God also then gave me the gift to write and told me as He healed me, my words would help to heal others. For it is written in Romans 2:11 For there is no respect of persons with God. What He does for one is available to all.

When God told me I would write, it's like I grabbed my pen and pad and started to write. Back then, through my pain, I wrote and through my sadness, I wrote. I felt it was a better outlet then doing things that I couldn't take back or things that would turn out bad. So, I spent time sitting up in my room, writing down all my feelings. Even back then my faith in God began to also be a turning point to helping me see things in a different light. I begin to believe in the fact that before I was formed in my mom's womb he knew me as stated in Jerimiah 1:5. My faith helped me to make it through.

How I made it through relationships, was by ultimately learning self-worth. That was not always the case. Having a void in my life growing up, looking for love outward made me settle to make bad decisions. I wanted to be in love so much until I settled for putting up with the potential of who people could be, never actually seeing them become that person. Yet, I gave all my time, feelings, emotions and attention. I had to learn that I was important, that I couldn't get so wrapped up in what others said when they did not mean what they said. I've been emotional hurt by the words of individuals who only truly cared about themselves. I feel I was at a disadvantage of not being able to truly know what a healthy relationship was.

I had to learn that people would change when they wanted to. I tried hard to not allow the relationships to make me bitter. I needed to realize that there was not a lot that I could do to make people change if they didn't desire too. I had to get down to the core, of what was it saying about the way I thought about myself and what I allowed in my life. Was my need to be loved so important that I would allow myself to be treated bad and make bad choices repeatedly?

In between these times of trying to get through the overwhelming feeling of not feeling like anyone could see me. I decided to steal out of a department store, in my mind I was saying I'll show you, however, I had the money to pay for it anyway. I got caught, was taking to the jail, handcuffed to the bench, and I felt horrible. This was my first time ever doing something like this. I was trying to prove a point and screaming inside my mind like, do you see me? Then the situation ended up going away by the grace of God.

It took a little while, and God would always tell me that I deserved better. God spoke to me again and said that others may never validate you, but I choose you. So, stop trying to prove to them who you are and get their attention, I see you. During that time, I begin to change my mindset. I begin to pour positive words into my life that would wake up in the mirror and say I am smart, I am beautiful, I am deserving. I had to change all the negativity that was surrounding me and what I believed to help to raise my self-esteem. When I begin to learn to love myself, I was able to change my behavior and what I let happen in my life.

How I made it through was increasing my prayer life and pouring every lesson learned into my poetry books. I started to heal myself to know that I deserved the best out of life. I had to encourage myself, I had to start to choose me over other people. I had to stop being a people pleaser and start to focus on me, the Amazing person God saw on the inside of me. Throughout my journey, I had to learn to take responsibility for my actions and to choose better. I had to learn how to speak life to myself when no one else did. I had to learn that my life was so much better living and learning to love myself.

Once I decided to truly believe in the reason God placed me on this earth and devoting my life to helping others overcome obstacles with my books. It has been the most rewarding journey ever. I can encourage individuals who feel like they do have a reason to live to look at their life from a different perspective and give them hope to hang on. I can talk to young girls and help them to start to become emotionally stable and to raise their self-esteem. I have been able to travel around the world with my books, to encourage, empower and edify others.

I am truly humbled to be able to share the message of how I made it through, with others. Once I changed my mindset and became determined to make a difference it motivated me to keep going. I came from a small town in Mississippi; however, it has never determined where God can take me what I can achieve. I have always had God in my corner believing me and encouraging me. I am happy that I can pay it forward. When I was in high school, I remember meeting the late Dr. Maya Angelou and, in the moment, I had with her, I expressed how when I got older, I wanted to impactive lives, as she had done with all her wonderful works. She encouraged me then to continue.

My faith to believe that I could help me to keep moving forward allowed me to use my story of wanting to end my life made me want to live my life to produce better. I learned over the years that not every day will be perfect, but if you can find one thing to be happy about then that's all you need. Throughout my life the major lessons that God was and has always been saying to me, is to be who He has created me to be. Each day I affirm who I am, love on myself and put my best foot forward. At this point in my life, I am doing just that because I am Fearfully and wonderfully made.

LaDonna Marie
www.ladonnamrie.org

JACQUELINE CARTER
Life after Eleven/She was only Eleven

The Saturday night that changed the lives of 6 children. I was the 5th child who faced the pain of losing my mother at a very young age. When it first happened, I really didn't realize what was really going on, until days begin to past by and my mother was not around and there were no more phone calls. My mother was the oldest daughter of 14 children born to my grandmother (Bettie). Out of the six children, only 2 were adults. This left my grandmother to step up and raise me and 3 of my sisters. I never imagined life without my mother, although she was a single (widow) mom raising 6 daughters. During the times back in the 1960s and early '70s, it was common to have single moms raising her children. My mother never made us feel that we were a burden to her, because of her marital status. She was a hard-working mother who vowed to make sure that her children had the best life. Although raising children can be rather challenging, my mother never showed us that life was challenging having to take care of her children. Unlike the others, I was a daddy's girl and always wanted to be with my dad. One day my mom decided to drive me to Chicago to live with my father and his wife at the age of 7 years old. Again I never imagined my life without my mother, four years had gone by and I remember talking to my mother on the phone she said: "I know I didn't send you anything for your birthday, but you will see me soon and I will have something for you then." As a kid when your parents tell you something promising, nothing else matters because, in my mind, I knew that I was going to see my mom soon along with a birthday gift.

One Saturday night May 24th, 1975 the doorbell ranged, it was my aunt (my mom's sister) who lived in Chicago, who came to bring me the news. I was 11 years old at the time, I remember being in the kitchen washing dishes when she arrived. My aunt looked at me with tears in her eyes, and her eyes were blood red and told me, your mother was just killed". At first, I didn't understand what she was telling me, because I had just spoken with her a few days ago and all I could hear was her voice telling me "you will see me soon"! The thought of what my aunt was telling me never registered in my mind. Days went by and I'm trying to process this, I never imagined life without my mother here. Just think of being eleven years old and lose your mother over an unhealthy relationship. Yes, I said an unhealthy relationship. You know when a man tells you, "Oh baby you're mine", then go to another woman's house and tell her the same thing. Living in the south women don't take the fact that their man is not only dating you, but he's dating someone else too.

Two weeks before this happened the other female and her sister decide to break into my mother's home looking for her shared man, to find out that he wasn't there. At that time my mother had the opportunity to take matters in her hands, but because of the type of woman she was and the kind heart she had towards God's people chose not to. Weeks later they returned to my mother's home catching her outside talking to this guy, when my mother turns around, she stabbed my mother in her heart. My mother runs into her house facing her 14-year-old daughter and 5 years old baby along with two grandchildren to try to retaliate but begin to lose strength. The neighbor across the street ran over to take my mother to the hospital, but after saying a few words to her 14-year-old daughter she died in her lap.

Over 44 years gone by since we lost our mother. Let me just share the kind of mother we had. Yvonne was the oldest daughter, the second child of 14 children she exemplified character among her siblings that whatever you do, be great in doing that. She also kept up with her mother Bettie, making sure her wardrobe and other essential things were always together. Although my mother was a widow, she took the initiative to yet raise her 6 daughters and teaching them to always strive for greatness, and not to allow anyone to dictate your destiny and give life all you have. She was stern on us becoming women and teaching us the importance of cleanliness, making sure that just as you dress fly, the inside of your house should be fly as well. My mother never left her house not being well put together. She made sure that her house was ALWAYS put clean. We weren't allowed to do anything in our "living room" but walkthrough because the living room was white carpet with white lavishing furniture entirely. She was worked for one of the riches white families in the city who owned a very upscale clothing store. Her boss kept her wardrobe tight, giving her the opportunity to showcase their clothes. In return, to draw attention to their store. Her personality complemented the clothing she wore. The two oldest sisters were 19 & 21 years old; they were very close to our mother as she yet gave them great advice to help aid them in being successful women and mothers when she felt there was a need too.

All 6 of our lives were shifted. My grandmother came to Chicago, moved me back to Mississippi to be with my other 3 siblings and raised the four of us. At that point in my life, I felt that was the right thing to do, realizing that we needed each other. My grandmother opened up her heart and home to raise her 4 grandchildren, even after all her children were grown. She stated she wouldn't have it any other way. Although my grandmother had two of her adult sons living with her, she made adequate room to house us.

Living in a household with a senior citizen who was set in her ways, we were young girls still trying to process all of this. "Why"? My grandmother was very dedicated in church. Before the church lights came on, we were at church. She took us to EVERYTHING, including choir program, deacons' program, pastor anniversary, motherboard program and more. We were burnt out with so much church, as we got older, we no longer wanted to go so much but living in her household you had no choice. Even as years went on, we were still disturbed about life without our mother. Eventually, every one of us began to demonstrate issues within ourselves without realizing that we needed counseling and or some help. During this time African Americans didn't believe that it was such thing as counseling, but honestly, we needed therapy and counseling.

Later on, my sister and I were teenagers/young ladies and felt that some of the directions and training that my grandmother gave were overboard. Then our rebellious behavior began to kick in. Actually, we just were not happy with life and wanted to do something different. We begin to open up to different people in the church about how we felt. They were the only people we would see going to church all the time. They began to take us places with their children to give our grandmother a break. Although she didn't see a need for that, all she said was NO to everything. At that point, I felt the urge to start voicing my opinion and of course it created a problem. My uncles felt it was time for them to take matters in their hands to discipline us. This was not good. My third oldest sister disagreed. My uncle would try to whip me. He would call us out of names and speak negative things to us. One day my sister said "enough is enough" she gave him the worst whipping a female could ever give to a man. Looking back over the years she was a caring person but had built up a lot of anger due to life without her mother. That moment some things needed to be released. Just imagine, living a life without your mother and no one never saw a need to get the 4 of us counseling. To this day I am affected by those things. I am leery about certain relationships and I don't tolerate confusion and many other things. I'll say life wasn't always bad. my grandmother gave us what she knew, and I appreciate her for that. All she wanted was to make sure we knew Jesus, and not have any babies at a young age. All 4 of us gave our life to Christ and were active in the church. But yet we still had a pain that we were carrying on the inside.

No matter, others begin to embrace us, but NO ONE could fill the void of my Mother. We grew up, graduated from high school and college, none of us were on drugs or alcohol. We remember the value and goals our mother instilled in us and applied those principles in our lives and with our children. Till this day I have moments, I share with my two daughters why I go that extra mile to be there for them because I didn't get that opportunity with my mother. The pain of losing your mother at the age of 11 years old is unexplainable, just know that you're blessed. And my life will NEVER be the same.

Jacqueline Ramsey-Carter

PAMELA STONE
From Bruised to BOLD

Hearing that ole childhood mantra sticks and Stones my break my bones, but words will never hurt me. Who made that up? Words will never hurt me, that's a lie. We need to teach our kids when called a name don't ignore the name-calling. It needs to be addressed. Stop bullying. Any who, see I've been called Big Mama, one I am not your mama. Then called Big Girl, when back then I should have said I got your Big Girl. Down to being laughed at. Man looking back now, I should have made my own comedy show and got paid. However, I let the name-calling affect me and society labels get the best of me which led me to weigh 400 pounds. How did I get to the lowest point of my life, food? Let's be honest, food don't call you names or laugh at the way you look or even make animal sounds at you. Damn, I really do have a comedy show. Hmmm, what should my show be called? Oh, sorry I lost focus.

Let me introduce myself my name is Pamela Stone I am a DeClutter your Life Life Coach, Business Development Coach, Speaker, Author, and Talk Show host. Declutter Your Life program was birthed due to my bruised life. Also, Because

I crossed paths with others, and they can't seem to move past the hurt. I have to say the pain allowed me to face everything openly. When facing the pain, man it was like stubbing my toe. An unforgettable pain. You know where you want to say a lot of sh** and cry at the same time. At the end of it all, I am able to smile at me.

The motivation to make a change was one day I got a nudge or a poke, but no one was around. I was like that really didn't happen, so I ignored it. Then the nudge or poke got a little harder. The one that gets your attention. Then I knew who it was, it was God. There is only one person that knows your purpose and your motivator. He told me to get up you got one life to live. And is he soon right so let me tell you how to SOAR to your purpose in 4 steps.

Step 1: S Self-care. Yes, I journal and yes, I meditate but my best self-care is retail therapy. Retail therapy to me is window shopping. I normally do this therapy by myself. Set 30 minutes aside every week and put it on my calendar for accountability.

Step 2: O Open to new Opportunity. So many of us keep putting this off. This step can lead to many hidden jewels. Here is where I found writing is not as bad as I thought. My love for reading bloomed here too.

Step 3: A Asses your assets and use them for your purpose. How many of us are good writers, good speaker's hell even good cooks? Use those talents, don't take them to your grave. Could you imagine where we would be without post-it notes or even cell phones? I would not say lost; we would move slower. Hey now, maybe that is what society needs. Slow down and enjoy life a little more.

Step 4: R Rise up. Turn I can't into I can. This step is time to rally the tribe together and get them behind you. Now, if you don't have a tribe, you reach out to my tribe called Conversate with Pamela. Conversate with Pamela can be found on Facebook. There is accountability and support.

So yes, the bruises from life tripped me but the 4 steps to SOAR were the starting point of me having a BOLD life.

This bold life has come with determination and an unstoppable attitude. So, I have made peace with food. By knowing food is not my enemy. I've changed my food choices by not eating fast food, not eating fried food, heck I don't eat meat.

Understand those were my triggers to 400 pounds. I love to walk and go to the gym as well. I've even done 5k walks throughout the year.

Not only that, but I also speak to young ladies and women around the world to go after their lives. Don't let the word NO, I CAN'T, and please don't let age stop you. And do it all in humor and a smile on your face.

Now don't get me wrong, I'm not perfect. I do have those moments. When I do, I just head myself back to one of the 4 steps to SOAR (up above).

In closing, I tell everyone. If I can do it, so can you!!!

Peace and Blessing
Pamela Stone, your DeClutter your Life Life Coach

SHELLY LEE
Fear Does Not Live Here Anymore

I was attending college for the first time. I was a 20-year-old college freshman. I was also heartbroken. See, the relationship with my first love, my high school sweetheart had ended. He cheated on me with someone who was very sexually promiscuous.

I had to pay for tuition/housing. I had been all over campus. I decided to go to my dorm for a break. While walking, I noticed this University worker breaking his neck looking at me. Smiling to myself I said "break your neck" as I ran up the stairs to my room to freshen up. I was thinking, Lord please don't let this man be lurking around waiting for me. I sat down to eat a snack. I had to head back out to finish the rest of my enrollment. I had received 2 scholarships from my high school; my tuition, books, and housing were paid for. I will admit that I worked hard to get to this point. I had Perfect Attendance from the 9th through the 12th grade and I received recognition during my graduation. My high school gave me a gold necklace and a leather Newton Eagle watch.

As I prepared to head out, I scanned the perimeter to make sure that the guy was not around. I proceeded downstairs. As I walked, I was thinking about the last bit of business I needed to handle before my day was over. I walked along the sidewalk and a male voice hollered "move over". I turned around and hollered "you can go around" as I kept walking.

I realized it was the University guy from earlier. He turned off the engine and said, "How can a guy like me get with a nice lady like you?"

Smiling because it was corny, I said, "I don't know."

He said, "May I have your number?"

I gave him my number and proceeded to leave. I thought you may call the number, but you don't even know my name.

Finally, I made it to my dorm room. The phone rings and it is him. He says," Can I speak to the lady I met on the sidewalk?

I disguised my voice and said, "She is not here."

Life went on and I did not hear from him for 2 weeks. Saturday evening, he called again.

I answered "Hello."

He said," Hi is the lady I met on the sidewalk?"

I laughed as I replied, "This is she."

He said, "How are you?"

I said, "You don't know my name."

He said, "You were rushing me."

We got to know each other. I told him that I was not interested in dating. high school sweetheart.

He told me that he was going to make me love him and he did.

Beaumont TX 1993

Barry's dad took us to the ER because I was having stomach problems. Diagnosis: 6 weeks pregnant. Yet Barry said he could not have kids.

We both wanted the baby. The bad news was telling my mother. Now mind you my mother was an old school mother. She could give you the look and you knew she meant business. If she called you by your first last and middle name, you better come quick. If she put her hands on her hips, you were about to be fussed at.

Crying, I called her on the phone. I said," Mama I got something to tell you."

She said, "Shelly what is it?"

I just sobbed.

She said, "You pregnant?"

I nodded my head even though she couldn't see me. I said, "Yes"

She said, "How many months?"

I got ready to answer but she said,"6 weeks?"

I said," Yes."

She said," Is it Keon or Barry's baby?

I said, "Barry."

She said, "Well Shelly, why are you crying? I am proud of you. You finished high school. You are grown and in college. I support you." Then I really started crying. I said, "Thank you, Mama." She said, "I am going to be a grandmother. My first grandchild." My daughter is now 9 months old. Now at this time, I had found out that Barry lied about his age. Instead of being 24 he was 26 and I was 21. I noticed that there was a certain car that would come, with a guy driving it. The guy would drive up. Barry would go outside. The car would leave. Barry would get all dressed up and say I will be back. After thirty minutes, the car would return but Barry was not at home. Hours later, Barry would return. I found out that Barry was a crackhead down through the years. I was never around this type of environment, so I did not know what to look for. He had been in and out of jail and in and out of rehabs.

DeRidder LA 2005

I told Barry it was over. I started seeing another guy. One day I came home from work and noticed that there was a footprint on my porch, and it wasn't mine. I unlocked the house door and left it opened as I slowly walked in. I kept my cell in my hand. Out pops Barry from the hallway, he had broken into my home. His sister had brought him a ticket from Houston to come down. I had a daughter and a son by Barry. Barry had me to tell my new man, Dennis, that it was over. I did but Dennis knew Barry's past. Barry kept an eye on us the whole time. He did not want us to leave the house. He fell asleep. I gathered some items and Dennis picked us up. We went to Shameka's house. I called my mother from a locked room. I heard a car door. I peeked out the window. It was my mother and my baby brother with a metal bat in his hand. I came out of the room and ran to my mother. I told Mama what transpired. My mother, brother and I went back to my house to get some clothes to stay with Shameka. Barry had torn down my Christmas tree, broken some pictures and a window. I reported it to the police and apartment manager.

    Dennis picked me up for work. The principal called me and told me that someone came looking for me at least five times. I told her about the situation. They put out an alert to not let Barry on the school grounds. The children and I are relaxing for the evening. Barry is knocking at the door. I called Mama first. She came, cursed him out, and took him to the bus station to go back to Houston. Barry came back again 30 min later. I don't know if the crack had him going or what, but he was ruthless. I called Mama and she cursed him out again and told him to stay his so and so at the bus stop. I did not hear from him, but I felt that he was still in DeRidder.

I went to work the next day and then to Shameka's. The police to escort me home. I gave the officer my housekeys. I stayed in the back of the police car. They went in and found Barry hiding under the bed.

Beaumont TX 2006

I am now living in Beaumont TX because Barry wanted to start over. I was going out of town to visit my mother. I returned three days later and found everything gone. Barry had broken in and stole my TVs, my gospel tapes, my iron, my son's Dub City cars, my daughter's bike, all the food out of the freezer, my iron and my electric can opener. I went to my apartment manager the next day to report it. I put the little belongings Barry had on the back porch. Nightfall, Barry came by and tried to get in through my daughter's window. I armed myself with butcher knife in one hand and cell phone with 911 already on screen. He wanted to talk at the back door. I kept the screen locked and the main door locked. I told him that it is over! I began to hate and pray Barry away. How can you pray and hate someone at the same time? Nightly, I would check all the windows and doors while armed with cell and butcher knife. I would sleep armed. I would go to the bathroom, armed.

One day I got a phone call from his sister. She said, "Shelly, Barry is in jail."

I said, "Are you serious?

She replied, "Yes."

I hollered, "Thank You, Jesus!"

See from July 12, 1993, to 2006 Barry had taken so much from my children and me. He had stolen 5 TVs, a refrigerator from an apartment complex, 1000s of dollars, video games, movies, groceries, my class ring, and my mother's ring. Anything that could be sold for $5 or higher he had taken. He had stolen from his family members. He was like a plague that destroyed everyone he encountered. Barry had stalked me. Barry had put his hands on me twice. Once he tore my dress down the middle and tried to drag me out the room naked because he thought I was showing myself to his friend. Another time he had my 10-yr. old daughter on the floor slapping her face because she had got smart with me. My 8 yr. old son came to get me. My son had jumped on Barry's back to get him off his sister and Barry slung him into a wall. I rescued my son. Then I got Barry off my daughter. Her cheeks were red. I called the cops and he was made to leave. Another time he had been going through withdrawals and no one was home but his nephew, me and him. Barry started calling me a bitch and saying that I ruined his life. He slapped me and told me to get out. I ran to the phone to call his sister. He snatched the phone. I ran outside to safety without any shoes. He kept calling me names and accused me of sleeping with an 18-yr. old. By this time, his sisters and my children had returned. The sisters grabbed me as I told them what occurred. Also, the guy in the car was a drug dealer. Barry was supposed to be selling the drugs but instead, he was using the drugs. My Thank You Jesus was warranted.

Back to the story, the sister said that Barry had gone to a house where the garage door was a few feet off the ground. Barry slid under there to see what he could take. The owner found him and made him get on the ground and held him at bay armed with a big pitchfork. The owner called the cops and Barry went to jail.

Down through the years, I learned that his family members knew that he had this addiction. No one thought it was important enough to tell me. I guess they thought let Barry be her headache now. Let her deal with him they must have thought. I also learned that Barry had been in jail 34 times before I met him. Some charges were for family assault, assault, drugs, and theft. When I had first looked at his record none of this info was available. Later I was able to find out who, what, when, where, and how.

So today I thank God for deliverance from Barry and fear. Now I am very observant. I know what signs to look for when it comes to crack substance abuse. I still check the doors out of habit. With the help of God, I am recovering all that what was taken from my children and me. God still has His hands on my children and me!

Real Divas Win ™ Volume #2

AYANA MICHE'
Concrete Rose

Born in the hottest month of the summer of '85 in Chicago, a seed had been planted. She didn't know it yet but, life was going to be one of the things she feared as a kid, A great big rollercoaster. Since she could walk, talk, and remember, she endured life's obstacles. As a child, her innocence had been tainted. All throughout her childhood she was bullied, talked about, teased, and dismissed. The dirty girl in school, nappy head, black, skinny, and unwanted human being. She didn't have what the other kids had. Sometimes she didn't even have what was needed; toothbrush, soap, clean underwear, deodorant, hell food even. You ever had sleep for breakfast, lunch, dinner, and snack? She bounced around a lot growing up; cars, shelters, basements, homes of others, and hotels were her home.

She was every name in the book except a child of God. They hated her; the fact that she was even born. They had no problem telling that to her face either. "Sticks and stones may break my bones but, words can never hurt". Who came up with that saying? Those words DID hurt. Damaged her to the core.

Kids can be so cruel. They don't know or even care what you're going through. Everything is funny to them. They just see the things that you don't have like them. Sounds of the children ringing in her ear singing "...Yo mamas on crack rock". Pointing and laughing at her. She always walked around with her head held down. Ashamed and always feeling blah. She often questioned her purpose in life. She felt ugly inside and out. She just knew God had made a mistake. You couldn't convince her otherwise. Only people paying attention to her were dirty old, perverted men. Blood or not. It didn't matter. Oh my! How They lusted for this little girl. Trying to lure her across the street to the hotel that catered to the prostitutes and dope fiends. She was only twelve. The streets were no good and were never lenient to anyone of age and/or circumstance. Anyone that was brought up in Chicago KNOW how the streets were.

Being a teenager was hell. A new city with new people. She was already an introvert. Being a people's person was never really her thing even though she would try at times. The teens had already started having sex. Some of them had kids. But who wanted me? Here I was with period bumps on my nose looking like a damn crystal ball. Skin oily as hell. Don't nobody wanna talk to me looking like that. The only good part of my teen years was that the seed had started to sprout. My breast was poking out, booty, thighs. I no longer looked like an ironing board. I got tired of being talked about for my hair not being combed so, I learned how to do my own. Braiding hair had become a thing. I got my first clients at only fifteen. The little funds started rolling in. I was able to make sure we had food sometimes. I had clothes, shoes, etc. I developed OCD when it came to hygiene products. I made sure I had what I needed and some. Taking hour-long showers and baths. One little drip of sweat and I'm back in the bathroom bathing.

People started to pay just a little bit of attention to me. Well, of course! I was the chick getting people heads right and making a little money. I started having sex, smoking, drinking, and hanging out; typical teenage stuff. The guys started looking because that seed had blossomed. Still in all they didn't want to be with her. They only lusted for her cause "Face wise, she ok" as they would say. I wasn't light enough for them, I just had enough ass for them to look at.

Around the time I started doing hair, I also started writing. I would talk to people and hang out sometimes but, deep down inside I still felt like that lonely little girl that wasn't good enough, pretty enough, or had enough. The struggle was real and I was quickly giving up on myself. The drinking became heavy. I started on half pints and worked my way up to a half-gallon by myself. I was all laughs around others but, when night fell and I was all alone, the demons would taunt me. I wanted to die. I couldn't fathom the fact I hadn't done anything wrong except for being born. Why was I enduring so much pain? Going through so much shit? What was my punishment? My questions weren't being answered. Over and over I asked God why? But I don't think he heard me. The writings in my journal became darker than the midnight hour.

Describing my every thought, nightmares, and my childhood years that left me tarnished. My words developed a rhythm. They started rhyming. Page after page I wrote about how I would take my own life, how much I hated myself, my looks, and my body. All I ever wanted to do was write, model, help people, design clothes, and do music. Every step I took forward was like a hundred steps back. The only thing that kept me going was my kid. I couldn't be selfish and leave him motherless. God knew what he was doing.

I didn't finish high school because I was still bouncing around a lot; City to city. Had I not had my son I'm almost positive I wouldn't be here. I wouldn't have made it see 21. I got my GED, Associates, and my bachelor's degree all by the time I reached my late 20's. In the midst of my storm, I still tried climbing those mountains but, oftentimes I wanted to give up. I felt defeated. My faith was deteriorating, my soul was damaged. I had grown angry at God. I doubted him; I was pissed. No matter how hard I fought on those battlegrounds it seemed as though it wasn't enough. I lost so much stuff over the years. Sadly, I had lost myself. People had done me so dirty over the years, blood AND water. WHAT DID I DO? WHEN DID I DO IT? I couldn't pray to or believe in a God that I had felt left me out to die. He gave me a story to tell but, I got tired of telling it. I wanted to share my victory, not my sorrows. Busting my ass felt like for nothing. I couldn't help but feel like a slave getting whipped just because. I'm not the one to pity anyone including myself so, as hard it was, I kept trucking along. I got tired of always just getting by, having faith the size of a mustard seed, and always crying. I already felt ugly. I didn't want to keep contributing to it. I felt as though God had abandoned me. No church or no prayer could help me during that time. My spirit was destroyed. That little girl in me was not at peace. The nightmares and the hauntings wouldn't stop. Seemed as though I just couldn't get a break.

A single mother, entrepreneur, student, hairstylist, a counselor on the side, a friend, cook, and a writer was all her. People looked at her as a phenomenal woman. "What can't she do?" they would often ask. That wasn't what she saw every time she would look in the mirror though. She saw a person who had been beaten spiritually, mentally, and emotionally. She saw someone who had lost faith and all hope.

At the end of her twenties, she had looked back at her life and realized God had never abandoned her. He was there holding her hand the entire time. Even when she gave up on him, he NEVER gave up on her. Her faith in him grew bigger than a mustard seed. The prayers got stronger and she couldn't thank him enough. She was able to put that little girl inside of her at peace and move forward. She began to love who she was inside and out and except the things she cannot change. Is she perfect? Absolutely not. Does she slip and slide? Yes. She's human. My trials in life were all part of the plan for where I am now.

Fear had me sitting for three years until I met up with a childhood friend of my siblings who found out I was a writer and pushed me out of my comfort zone. He introduced me to an AMAZING publisher and writer, Ms. Tiffany Green who saw more in me than I had seen in myself. I am forever humbled. Now here I am getting ready to release my first book "Life as a Trend" A book of poems in March 2019. When you let go and let God handle things that you shouldn't even put a finger on, the impossible becomes possible. Through the dirt, up the concrete, sits a beautiful rose!

www.ayanamiche.info

LATOYA MOORE
Broken Pieces

As I sat and watched the ink hit the paper of my mother's birth year until that present moment where I was standing, my body fell numb. My thought process was non-existent and my ability to register what was taking place became harder to comprehend.

1949 to 2014- I refused to accept it. I followed through the process but already concluded in my head that my mother was on an extended vacation far, far away from her place of residence on Michigan Ave in Chicago, IL. I was just with my mother at the movies on that Sunday evening watching 22 Jump Street starring one of her favorite actors, ICE Cube. No sickness, no sudden fever, no allergies, no nothing. We laughed and had a ball just the day before. What in the hell happened? Life happened.

This is why I felt it was imperative that I share my story with you as our journeys may be different, but our obstacles to getting through to the next day are quite similar. It's like a war without the artillery. We're out in the field with no protection because sudden situations strike with no warnings- just like missiles and bombs. It's hard to cope as humans when devastation hits because we never wake up expecting our lives to change. My world changed forever the moment my mother took her last breath. Not only was she my best friend, but she was my biggest supporter, my "Go to" when things didn't work out, my doctor, my counselor, my caretaker (spoiled), and my 1st Love.

So, how can I get passed this excruciating pain?

I was mad, I was livid, I was so terribly hurt for myself and other's that my mother touched that I began to replay over and over in my head- what could I have done differently to help save my mother. I kept coming up with the same answer. NOTHING!

At this point, I had to do exactly what my mother would have wanted. I had to confront my pain head-on so that I could drown the residue of agony with something worth living for. I had to find my true purpose. I wrote a book that my mother had the pleasure of sharing the experience 9 months before her passing and when I say that was one of theeeeee best feelings in the world. Not only was it a packed house at my book release celebration, but my mother thought she was co-author because she walked around and greeted guest as if she wrote the book (LOL). I loved it though.

All I ever dreamed of was her seeing me standing in my truth and doing what I loved, and God provided me that platform before my Angel departed.

Turning Point

In the last couple of years, I've been trying to rediscover myself. I've decided to turn the light switch back on because I got tired of sitting in the dark. I had to realize that my mama didn't raise no punk! Therefore, I had to get off my ASS and do exactly what she would have wanted me to do and that's LIFE!

So, let's talk for a second. What have you allowed to stifle your growth into greatness? Yes, you sis?

Are you battling with the constant disappointment's life throws your way? Are you fed up? Hell yeah, I know I am. So, what are we going to do about it? I say let's began to start throwing the bullSh$% back and take back our lives no matter how hard the burdens are. Think about it, we will never be free from pain, disappointments, sorrow or having the luxury of nothing ever happening to us. It's impossible. But what I do know is how we can start rotating our displeasures and turning them into the greater good. We have to reprogram our brains to work through the emptiest places in order to become our best selves. Once we have this mastered, we have become unstoppable. We have to be able to pull greatness even from a glass that's half empty. But how sis? You ask.

Most of us are battling so much that we allow our future to be threatened by the joy snatchers (People, Pain, imPossibilites, imPerfections and old Patterns). Instead of drinking from a cup of Poor habits, how about we replace the 16th letter of the alphabet with the 4 Positive P's- Passion, Purpose, Perseverance, and Possibilities.

It's all about how we train our minds to see the good versus the bad.
-Are you willing to let that business idea fall to the wayside because of doubt and uncertainty?
-You've been through so much that you just want to get through the day with a sane mentality? WE ARE ALL GOING THROUGH SIS! No one is exempt!

Let me share with you how I turned things around to work for me.

I took a break- PERIOD'T

I sat still for 3 whole years to gather my thoughts and to grasp the concept to function like a normal human being again.

I had to inhale-exhale-inhale-exhale (also known as) BREATHE!

NO, I did NOT think it would take me 3 years to find my glow again. It was an assignment from God to sit still with no specific time frame.

LaToya's plan was to sit for 6 months to a year to focus solely on the well-being of my health, mental and state of existence, but God had another completely different agenda.

Broken Pieces

The year was 2015, I've just broken off my engagement to someone that I was in love with because I repeatedly kept seeing the same recycled habits being displayed towards me and I got tired of that shit. I had to make a conscious decision to let go and LET GOD! I literally did this, but it was nowhere near easy.

Here I am mid 30's, thinking I've found my prince yet turned out to be just another lesson before the blessing. 2014, I just said good-bye to my mother and now this. My sixteen-year-old son at the time is now acting out in ways unimaginable. Suspended from school, ditching, fighting, smoking weed, becoming rebellious and I have no manual handbook to tell me how to get out of this rough patch in my life. My son lost his dad to a motorcycle accident back when he was only six years old, so I'm STUCK, LOST AND felt completely ALONE. When going through the Rocky Mountains, we never stop to give ourselves credit because we are still in the midst of the fire. Have you ever looked back on your life and thought to yourself- How did I get through that? Almost as if you were carried and placed on the other side of HOPE! That's all I had was that. HOPE!

You think what I just shared was bad, but it got worse. I don't want to go too deep into details, but let's just say some friendships were tested, lost, revealed and a list of other things. At one point, I had to look myself in the mirror and just laugh while crying. THIS CANNOT BE MY LIFE!

Bam. I'm done. In August of 2015, I decided to sit. I didn't want to date, no new friends, no refurbished relationships- nothing. I didn't want anything from anyone. I just wanted what we all want and that's PEACE OF F@#&ING MIND!

I walked through life for 3 years as if I wore a black veil over my entire body and face. No one could see me. I didn't get asked out on dates, no flirting, no feeling pretty, no nothing for that first year and a half. I was confused. I was like God really? It wasn't until year #2 where I began to understand my journey, but it was still a struggle to fully grasp because I was the only one at that time feeling the way I felt without a book on what these symptoms meant.

I had my sister, my true friends, and my sanity to get me past this dark place that I was in. After praying and more praying I began to understand my sudden disconnection from the world.

God placed me exactly where he wanted me to be- out of sight of distractions, misleading relationships, biased situations, and a list of other things that screamed ISOLATION.

Even though I was in an incubator to restore what was broken, I never once felt a sense of depression or unhappiness which was weird, but I did feel empty.

I became more cautious of my surroundings and where I placed my energy and very particular of other people's exchange of energy.

Year #2 I began to embrace the space that I was in. I was okay with letting people know that my cookie pie would be left in the cookie jar until the right cookie man came around that will appreciate the cookie, lol- If you know what I mean.

I was so serious. My friends would ask if I was deprived of it or how can I go so long without it, blah, blah, blah. I knew they were just being my crazy friends, but this was not their journey- it was mine. Therefore, trying to bring understanding to others that never had to cross this bridge would be only draining to the soul and cause confusion and unhealthy responses that would place strain on good relationships. So make the conscious effort to either keep things to yourself or to only share with those that may have an understanding of what it is you're going through.

Ask God to place you around those that are going through a similar situation.

So, here's the conclusion. Year 3, the year of the WIN 2018!
I had a renewed respect for myself. At this time, I am certain that God had me on this path for a reason. The veil began to come off and I began to be seen again. This time by the right individuals and opportunities. I finished and released book number 2 called "With Yo UGLY Self", a book based around

our insecurities and unhealthy habits. My book release was a success, I began to date again, new relationships were being built and believe it or not, my extremely picky self actually liked someone that is truly amazing.

Doors on top of doors began to open. Fear is no longer an option FAITH is now my best friend. I take more chances because I would rather fail multiples times, change my approach, start over from a different angle then to ever face the pain of regret and giving up. I wasn't built that way and neither are you.

The enemy wants us to believe that we are stoppable and he/she will do anything to go about making that happen. It is up to us to mutilate every punch that's thrown that has every intention of breaking us.

My weapon of choice is the love I have for my beloved mother. Her love for me is all I need to carry on. No, she's not here in the flesh, but she's definitely with me in spirit and I feel her presence daily.

Therefore, let us no longer embrace defeat, but welcome possibilities to a world that's big enough to fulfill everyone's dreams and goals. Let us no longer look to the left of emptiness, but look to the right of ambition and determination to get things done no matter what headspace we are in.

CLEANSE+CREATION=COMPLETION.

Sometimes we have to first cleanse our soul to create greatness in order to accomplish completion. Let's get it!

MARICE WILSON
Sometimes You Have to Lose to Win Again

No one ever wants to talk about losing. Let's face it, losing sucks! It makes you feel bad. It makes you start doubting yourself, your dreams, your other accomplishments and ultimately, your self-worth.

Where shall I begin….

Just when I thought my life was on the upswing because my marriage had been revived (you can read my story of how 30 days of positive communication transformed my marriage in my bestseller, Journey to Love.), I was hit with a tsunami. I was swept up and I couldn't swim fast enough to get out. The thing about a tsunami is it comes with little warning. You don't have much time to run for shelter or find higher ground. You cannot detect when it will begin, and you do not know how many waves will come. You immediately go into survival mode because at this point; it's either sink or swim.

I decided to swim.

In 2014 was my first wave. The previous year my husband and I committed to loving each other and to building our marriage. Life was going well, we were parenting our children, the ministry was prospering, and we were working on our goals. Then my husband gets the call from his sister that his mother is now terminally ill and the care of her would take more than she was capable of handling. Now comes the dreadful and hurtful decision of where to place mom. We tried taking her back and forth to each of the sibling's homes to share the load (keep in mind that his sister and mom lived in another state 3 hours from us) but with children, work, ministry, and life; it became overwhelming. Plus, the care she needed required professional help. They could no longer avoid the inevitable, we were not equipped to handle her needs; so, reluctantly she had to be placed in a nursing home. This alone is devastating. Throughout this process, I had to be there for my husband. When I had my own personal feelings or wanted attention, I had to step back and give him the space to deal with it. He spent most weekends traveling to see his mom. Some days she knew he was there, other days she didn't. When he asked me to ride with him to see her, I dropped what I was doing so that I could be with him. He needed a friend.

The second wave came in 2015. As Fred's mom's health continued to decline, I found out that my mom was diagnosed with pancreatic cancer and it was terminal. Nobody prepares you for this kind of news. There is no class to take to prepare you for this part of life. So, while Fred was taking care of his mother; I along with my siblings, began the journey of taking care of my mother. I prayed for a miracle! I believed God would turn it all around and make both moms well and vibrate. I reminded God of all the good I had done and that "He owed me". Sounds crazy huh. I told God that so many people needed to see a miracle and my mom, a woman who gave her entire life to Christ and His work deserved this Miracle! Fred's mom had sacrificed for ministry and she was his child, and she should be next in line for her miracle. I tried to bargain with God. Despite my pleas, prayers, and begging, God did not rule in our favor. In September of 2015, we laid my dear mother-in-law to rest. I know that dying is a part of the life cycle, but it doesn't make it hurt any less. We now had the daunting task to explain death to our children while reminding them that God's grace was sufficient. We had lost the matriarch of my husband's family. My kids had lost a grandmother and if I'm honest, I had lost a little bit of our faith. We wanted to see a miracle, but God wanted his child to be with Him.

The third wave didn't give us much time to regain my strength. We really didn't have time to mourn because I had to go right back into caring for my mom. Her cancer began to ravage her body and I watch this once vibrant and full of life woman be reduced to skin and bones. The hardest thing I ever had to do was watch my parents die. The daily trips to the oncologist, radiologist, primary doctor, and blood work were all-consuming. My siblings and I shared the load, but it was still too much to bear. It's amazing how one mother can take care of five children, but it takes five children to care for one mother. But we did it. We coordinate our schedules, put things on hold, missed our own appointments just to be there for mom. It was daunting, yet a privilege.

We made it through the rounds of chemo and radiation and prayed for God to show himself strong in our situation. I never doubted that He could do, I just wondered if He would do it. The doctor called my oldest sister and told her to bring mom in for a consultation and told her that it would be best if we all came. I wanted with everything in my power to believe that it was good news, but my heart knew different. As we all gathered in his office, we could see the sadness on Mom's face. We tried to cheer her up and remind her that God was still in control. We tried to use the same scriptures and pep talk she had given us so many times before. She looked up and gave us a half-smile and said, "It will be ok. You guys will be ok." and then she hung her head. Finally, the doctor came in. He had his poker face on, so I was unable to read him. He greeted us and complimented us on how we cared for her. That was the end of his small talk. He cut right to the point; straight, no chaser! He told us that chemotherapy nor the radiation worked. Her cancer was aggressive, and it wasn't anything else they could do. He offered another round of chemo, but that would only prolong the inevitable. He asked her if she wanted to try another round and my mom, in a small shaking voice, said "No! I'm tired." My brother then asked, "If she doesn't do chemo, how much time does she have?" The doctor didn't give us a definitive answer, he simply said, "Not long, so make every day count." After his last comment, he left the room to give us some privacy. A tear began to run down my mom's cheek, I tried to fight my tears, but was unsuccessful. I wanted to scream, but I needed to be strong for mom. I simply turned my head, wiped my face, put on my big girl panties and pulled it together. My oldest sister said, "Mom, you sure you don't want to at least try?" She didn't answer her, instead, she stood up, put on her coat and said, "Let's go!" The ride home was awkward and silent. No one could find the words to say, so we just turned on the music, rode in silence and enjoyed this time with mom. That day a little bit more of my faith died.

Two of my sisters lived in another state, so they were not there for the consultation. They gave me the task of calling and giving the update. Why they told me to do it, I will never know. I'm the baby and that day I was acting like it. I could not stop crying. So reluctantly, I called. I called my sister Shawinette in Atlanta first. She was sitting by the phone waiting. She answered on the first ring. I told her to hold on while I call Niecy on the three-way. She could hear the sadness in voice and demanded I tell her immediately what was going on. I told her I only wanted to say it once and clicked over. Now all three of us are on the phone and I began to give them the rundown of the doctor's prognosis. As I went on, I could hear weeping on the other end. Now that didn't help my cause at all, I was trying to fight my tears, but hearing someone else cry automatically makes me cry. So, on the phone, we wept together. After we cried and I answered all the questions they had to the best of my ability. Before the end of the day, they had purchased their plane, tickets and would be back in Chicago before the weekend.

Several years before, I had watched how my dad had deteriorated from cancer and ultimately had succumb to the disease. Watching my mom go through the same, brought back those images I thought were gone. It brought back the sadness of losing my dad and now I was losing my mom. I jokingly asked my sister Lynn, "If Mom dies, will we be orphans"? Everyone chuckled, but deep down inside, I felt that way. I felt robbed, my siblings had many years with both parents, and I only had a little time. Mad, hurt, jealous was an understatement.

A few months later, my mother slipped into a non-responsive state for 5 days. My siblings and I stayed in her house, taking turns watching her. Each day that I watched her, a little piece of me died. Would God raise her up as he had done for Jarius' daughter? (This story can be found in Matthew 9:18-26) Would He perform some miraculous healing? I prayed hard for a miracle!

I had to leave my mom's house to attend a conference that I had agreed to speak at months before. I don't know why I just didn't cancel. Since I had promised I would go, I did. After I spoke at the conference, I decided to go home to shower and take a nap. I hadn't slept in 5 days so exhausted was an understatement. As soon as I drifted off to sleep, my phone rang and my sister Niecy was on the other end. She said two words that would change my life, "She's gone!" I didn't respond with words, instead, I belted out a loud scream and began to weep. Fred was sitting right next to me. He didn't say a word, he simply held me in his arms and I wept. Six months after losing my mother-in-law, I lost my mother. The fourth wave had been the toughest wave to navigate. I thought this would be the wave that would take me out. I had no strength to swim. Now, as I look back, I now realize that I didn't have to swim because God was carrying me.

"God is our refuge and strength, an ever-present help in trouble."
Psalm 46:1

Losing two parents in one year is hard. I asked God if he could spread the pain out. Did we have to experience all in the same year? A few months after we laid my mother to rest, we found out that Fred's dad's cancer had come back. He had been a 10-year survivor and he was our poster child for healing. This time it came back with a vengeance. He was our last living parent and here we were, back at the beginning of what would be the end. While grieving, we are now back at doctors' appointments, parental care, chemotherapy, radiation, and uncertainty. I had a long talk with God. I was frustrated, tired, angry and sad. My father-in-law had been a pastor and literally gave his life to serving others and I could not understand why he had to suffer. And losing two parents was enough. God are you going to take everything?????? Wave five- dad didn't beat cancer this time. We lost all three living parents in 3 years. The pain and grief made me numb.

Someone snapped a picture of me while at the funeral and I noticed that a huge patch of my hair was gone. I can't tell you when it fell out and I certainly can't tell you how. I had been natural for over 10 years. I used the best shampoos and conditioners for natural hair. I would take hours to wash, detangle and twist. I would watch YouTube videos and took pride in caring for my hair and now it was gone. When I realized what was happening, I fell to my knees and cried, Lord what is happening!!!!!!! This sixth wave may seem vain, but to me it was devastating. From all of the stress, I was losing my hair and I didn't know what to do.

During all of the caring for our parents, burying or parents and trying to deal with grief, our ministry suffered. We had nothing to give. We didn't have the luxury of taking a three-month sabbatical. We thought we were being spiritual by "working" and "worshipping" through it. But inside we were dying. I did not grieve properly and as I look back; the church did not give us room to grieve. They allowed us to keep working and after a few weeks, expected it. You must take what you need instead of waiting on others to give it to you. People always say, "I'm here for you." But once the funeral is over and the food is gone at the repast, the compassion leaves. Life quickly went back to business as usual and each Sunday that I attended church, my body was there but inside, I was empty. I was leading while bleeding and no one even noticed. Because my husband and I were not operating at 100% of people begin to leave. Some felt they were "called" to attend another church and some just stopped coming. As a result, the ministry experienced a significant decline, and I lost my passion for ministry. It could have been a combination of grief and exhaustion, but it came at a cost. I thought this tsunami would never end! The waves kept coming.

I attended a Pastor's wives conference shortly after we buried my father-in-law. I thought being around other praying women would be good, but it actually made me feel worse. One of the speakers told the testimony of how God had healed her mom who was dealing with cancer. She told a very touching story of how her mom had served the Lord and how they came together and prayed for healing and ultimately, she was healed and went on to live several more years. I was mad! My mom, mother-in-law, and father-in-law served the Lord faithfully, we came together and prayed, and God did not heal! Before I knew it, tears were rolling. And I no longer wanted to be there. God sent reassurance that it wasn't personal. He loves all of his children and although I didn't get the outcome I would have liked that soon I would see that it was all working together for my good.

Then one day I could finally feel the ground under my feet. I could see the waves receding, the sun began to shine again and I could hear the voice of God clearer and He reminded me:

"No, despite all these things,
overwhelming victory is ours through Christ, who loved us"
Romans 8:37

Thank you, Lord, Not only do I have victory, but I had an Overwhelming victory! I am reminded of Job- He had many tragic things happen to him consecutively and after it was over, he was blessed with more! I am now experiencing my MORE! I had to go through it, so I could GROW through it!

This was my personal journey; yes, it had valleys but after a valley comes a mountaintop. Losing made me appreciate the wins! And when I decided to move from a pity party to rejoicing because of all God had done; and is doing; I won my independence. I was no longer crippled with sadness. I won a closer relationship with Christ because being low, forces you to pray and count on Him. I won a closer relationship with my husband and my sibling because tragedy forces you to depend on those you love. We became closer than ever. I won another chance to stop doing what no longer brought me joy and focus on what makes me happy. I am now brave enough to say no without explaining myself. and most importantly, I won my faith back. I get to see God work in my life.

"If I didn't have to explain my yes, I will not explain my no!"

Don't allow grief to steal your joy or blind you from seeing God work in your life. Don't allow others to dictate how you go through tough times. Your process is your process. I wrote a letter to all the people who I thought had abandoned me when I was at my lowest. I said everything I needed to say and then I deleted it. It felt good to get it out of my system, but later I realized that it would not stop them from being who they are, and it would not change the past. Since I no longer needed them in my life to reach my destiny, it was no need to waste any more energy on them. The letter helped me get it out and to no longer live in the past.

And always remember:
Tough times don't last; Tough people do!

God has a greater plan for my life and now that I can see clearly and I'm free I'm going after everything he has for me. Stay tuned because this story isn't over. I am one of a winning streak! When I won back my strength to keep moving forward, I have seen doors open, I have speaking engagements, book ideas, meaningful relationships, streams of income and peace of mind. Don't allow your losses to define you, instead, use it as a steppingstone to reach your destiny.

I am a winner!

Website/Blog/Store
MarcieWilson.com

Social Media
Facebook

Real Divas Win ™ Volume #2

Marcie Stowers-Wilson
Today's Leading Lady Facebook Group
Love Academy (for couples) Facebook Group
A Fresh Wins (page of inspiration)

Instagram
@MarcieWilson17
@a_fresh_wind

Twitter
@afreshwind

FOR BOOKING OR COACHING EMAIL ME
Marcie@MarcieWilson.com

NICHOLE STOKES SHARP
A Journey From My Soul to Myself:
Breaking the Silence

The new year brought what most would consider being good news and what would be thought to be a precious gift, a child. This is where I enter the cruelness and uncaring world surrounded and covered in lies and deep family secrets and no loyalty from anyone. Unsuspecting of what this journey would bring to me, I exist to some and am barely tolerated by others. Born to Rance Thornton and Ramie Warrenton, I am told that I just looked at my mom and didn't cry. My father was there when I was born and he was the one who named me, Nichole Lanez Thornton. Yall remember how the old westerns come on and the rolling tumbleweed would come across the town? Only thing is that nobody knew that sign meant that some mess or trouble was coming. It seemed like it followed me from the time I could walk and talk.

I would like to take you on a journey into my life that will let you see and know that being silent is dangerous and the truth must be told! Most stories and experiences should be sugarcoated to make others feel comfortable about what they won't confront, acknowledge or even believe. I came to break the silence that has lasted most of my life and the need to free myself from the bondage and baggage that has shaped my entire life from a child to through my adulthood. I can remember as far back as age 2, so that means that I have over 40 years of memories of my extraordinary life and they are good and bad but they are part of who I am but I now release them in my story so that my true destiny can emerge and I can help others. Starting when I was 4 years old, I was molested by the piano player, Harry at the church that I grew up in and I was about 6 when he stopped. I remember very distinctly the Irish Spring smell and his belt buckle and how he used to take me and my Lil sister to the park to play. I never got to play, because I had to play grown up with him. I learned how to kiss when I was 5 and how to lay on my back on the ground at 5 while he laid on top of me and smothered me with his weight. Nobody could see me, so it looked like he was just lying under the tree taking in the scenery! I was there and I existed, but he thought it was ok to do what he wanted to me and nobody ever caught on what he did except maybe his sister. Karen let my sister play, but I never saw anything happen to her, but she had to know what he was up to. The silence was not golden and if she had spoken up, he may not have been able to keep molesting other girls in the church and they were all ages but not old enough to really know what they should tell. Go figure! After him, the drummer, Jesse was next and I remember him too because he used to always have a big, swirly rainbow sucker and he gave it to me every Saturday at church. Everybody knows that when you give a child candy you have effectively distracted them and can basically do what you want right? He gave me the sucker because he had his hand in my panties from the back to the front and from the front to the back. I felt funny and uncomfortable and I would cry but all he did was try and rock me on his lap for me to be quiet so he can continue to play in my panties. Again, I was forced to kiss him like we were in a real relationship and that went on until I was almost 7 years old! Nobody ever picked up what he did either! I will never forget the feeling that something was confused as to why nobody these picked up that these bad things were happening to me. I also started writing at age 7 using my experiences and my imagination to write short stories, and after this second cycle of molestation, there was a gap for a about 3 to 4 years. At age 11, this last pedophile was a choir member who frequented the family gatherings at a relative's house on the weekends where there were at least 25 kids running around and playing everywhere. It was easy to target kids because it was so many, and folks were not paying attention. That is a smorgasbord for a pedophile because they will go undetected and he did. I remember that it was a Saturday and a lot of us were in the house watching WWF and I fell asleep on the couch in the living room. I don't know how long I slept but I know I opened my eyes and looked right in the eyes of Evan the choir member! He then put a sock in mouth so I couldn't scream and picked me up off the couch, threw me over his shoulder and carried in my sister's aunt basement to the bed that was down there! The bed was actually there because a cousin would get tore up drunk and that's where they used to put him to sleep off the alcohol. There in that creepy basement was where Evan's reign of terror started. I remember the belt buckle and him smelling like cigarettes and a weird smell. I was bit, and he kept me where I couldn't move but he put all his weight on me and he tried to penetrate me. He couldn't though. I was 11 to his about 24 years old and he was too big, but he kept trying but it wasn't working. I remember how he would always know where to find me and when I would go to the bathroom, but he would follow me, and he never stopped trying. I had no one to tell but my god-sister, Dayarra who was 8 or 9 years old! I used to cry on her lap, and she would rub my head and wipe my tears! Evan was relentless, it was so scary I was giving my candy money to my lil sister and her cousins to come to the bathroom with me so I wouldn't be by myself! He had two brothers Joey and Bobby that knew what he was doing so I was extremely terrified that they were going to run a train on me and I would be raped by all 3 of these pedophiles! I was scared that if they did that I would be killed! Every time Evan molested me, I would go to the bathroom at my sister's aunt's house and run hot water and pour bleach in the water to try and erase him off my body. The water was pink because he never stopped trying to penetrate by forcing himself but he wasn't able to so I was still hurt and ashamed. I was so ashamed and I didn't know what to do or how to say so I retreated into books and writing and I eventually started asking my mom could I stay with my God-mom, Lianna. When she said yes, I felt some relief but I was so stressed out and worried and for the next 25 to 30 years I would suffer from night terrors, insomnia, depression, and panic and anxiety and eventually thoughts of suicide too. The last cycle of molestation with Evan came to a complete stop one evening. I went upstairs to the bathroom and he followed me as usual but this time I was fed up and I ran into one of the bedrooms upstairs in the dark and grabbed the aluminum bat from behind the door. I waited and he came in that room on me and chased me around the entire bed trying to get at me. I swung and started yelling but this time my sister's aunt just happens to come up the stairs and came in that room where we were and turned the light on and asked what was going on? He couldn't answer so he lied and got out of the room but I stood there and I was looking wild about the eyes and I looked at her and told her that he was chasing me in that room. Nothing else was ever said. I survived at age 12 to 3 different cycles of child molestation committed by men in the church that were never caught, confronted or prosecuted. I went through my teen years feeling screwed up and abnormal and wanted to die every chance I got so I wouldn't feel the pain that I was feeling. I felt unloved and unwanted and felt like trash, I believed that if the pain would stop, I would be normal again. The emotional effects of child molestation and the trust in adults that was destroyed and 7 years go by and when I turned 18, the cycle with Evan came out but it was quickly buried because nobody wanted to bring a bad reputation or name to the church so it was never spoken of or addressed. I want to say that it wasn't ok to keep what happened silent so as to not embarrass people but there had to be other girls my age that may have been molested by these same 3 pedophiles but nobody broke the silence. As children, we are supposed to be able to tell the adults and they protect us but my voice was silenced but I hereby unmute myself because my voice mattered then and it matters now and I'm free! I owe it to those who don't have a voice and those who lost themselves and their lives in the midst of this inexcusable secret that kills and destroys lives! I have spent the majority of my adult life battling the demons that come with being molested: low self-esteem, self-hatred, self-destructive behavior, abusive relationships that can and often end up deadly. After my childhood devastation, I never healed from those cycles and I went into my teen and young adult years carrying those scars. At age 18, I entered into another level of abuse. I came from a strict Christian upbringing and I credit my mom for teaching me about God and the example she set. I learned that we were supposed to grow up get married and have babies, not go to college and make something out of yourself. I was bucking against that no lie. I wanted an education not a husband and kids but my goals were pushed to the back burner. It was in the summer at the start of my senior year in high school when I met the person who introduced me to Domestic Violence in a crash course. I met him in June of 1992 and in September 1992 we were married. I wasn't in love but the fear had been placed there from the start. It appeared that this is what I wanted but it was what he said to me for him to get what he wanted. Marry me now because nobody else will get you but me. I was naïve and had no clue that those were signs of controlling and manipulating behavior. I thought he must really care and wants this to be. Wrong it what it was. It was never about him wanting me it was a conquest for him, linking up with the desperate, homely looking and country dumb church girl that didn't know the first thing about how men do women or what to do with a grown man. He was 32 to my 18 so yes, he knew he had a green chic and was completely down for destroying my life. I take the blame for being naive and not knowing what it took to be with a man or even love him. Heck, I didn't even love me, so I was clueless on that one. Immediately I was isolated from friends and family except for his family. The abuse started immediately, and it was his rules, or it was no way. I had my first son when I was 19 and graduating from high school and went for my 6-week check-up and found out my second son was on the way. My body didn't heal from the first baby and by the time my second son was born I had been put on bed rest and the pregnancy was high risk. I dealt with medical issues that sent me to the ER on the regular and I actually went into labor at 6 months! After 2 years I was pregnant a 3rd time, but we were fighting and I miscarried. A week later I was pregnant with my 4th child.

By this time, I was in year 3 of Domestic Violence and I was regularly being abused. It started with the emotional abuse of the first pregnancy and it got worse every time I was pregnant. I was sodomized, tortured every day, being raped, fighting with him and I ended up running to the local shelters for help starting in October of 1997. I was granted my 1st Protection from Abuse Order against him. I tried to escape, and he told me that if he can't have me nobody can. There was nobody that wanted me because I had his kids and that I was dumb unless he told me what to say. I had to keep my head down and make no eye contact with nobody and walk behind him. I believe he hated me every bit as much as I hated myself for being with him. I didn't recognize the signs of abuse until it was almost too late. Between being threatened to get burned by the iron if I didn't wake up and argue or being choked until I passed out and wake up with clothes on sometimes naked or him sitting on my chest so I couldn't breathe knowing I had asthma or that my daughter was laying next to me because I breastfed her.

There was drug abuse happening and he tried to sell drugs but ended up using instead. We lived our life like NYPD Blue only my house never got raided and I didn't lose my children. There were drug dealers in our house bagging drugs at my kitchen table where I fed my children and guns in the house. I was given the choice to stay downstairs or go upstairs. I would choose upstairs so I could wrap my arms around my children and pray that we didn't lose our lives and I started praying to God for a way of escape. We were one of the new young families with 2.5 children and one on the way at the church we attended. Nobody suspected abuse or paid attention to the fact that I was wearing high collared blouses to cover up bruises and fingerprints on my neck. He was shouting from one side of the church to the other side and nobody ever called what was happening. He had drilled in my head that our business is our business so one Sunday he came to the church because he wanted me to stop the divorce. I said no and he backed me up on the hood of somebody's car and tried to put me through the windshield. It took about 6 brothers from church to pull him off me. Now everybody saw that incident and the truth was out now. I was 24 years old when I was able to break free and actually move from the house we lived in together. I remember on February 13, 1998, I was scheduled to go to a gospel concert with my church, but he decided that he wasn't going to watch the children so that I could go. His cousin volunteered and kept them for me, and I went to the concert. That night I got confirmation from God with the gospel hit "No Weapon by Fred Hammond and then again with "He's an On-Time God by Dottie Peoples. Armed with the answer from God, when we came back from the concert I stayed at a friend's house from church. The next morning, I wrote a note and told her that I would see her later and I walked to my house. I got closer and I had so much fear that sweat was running down my back that I had made my peace with if I had to die then my children won't find me. I started to memorize the scenery and looking around because he already stated that the only way, I was leaving him was in a body bag and to pick a day because he was ready. I had about 10 seconds to make my peace about dying because I didn't want to live like that and my children didn't deserve to live like that. So, I tried to save them by sacrificing myself and my life. After I got inside the house, I checked the entire house and then I deadbolted the locks and I stood in the middle of the kitchen and I said, "God you have to help me tell what to do" He said get the garbage bags from underneath the sink and fill them with the children's things. I started doing that and then there was a knock at the door. I froze I thought he was locked out again so I asked who it was and my lil sister was at the door, so I said who is it and he stated her name and I opened the door. She asked me what I was doing, and I told her that I was leaving. So, we worked together, and she took all the food out the cabinets and freezer. We loaded down a cab with about 6-8 garbage bags you use for the leaves and I went to my mom's house. I left everything in the apartment: furniture, suits and electronics and everything in between. At this time, I felt that the material possessions didn't matter if I was dying trying to get those things. I had courage and strength from God, so I moved forward. I stayed with my mom for 3 months to finish up my nursing certificate program and I got hired where I did my internship and took the job. I was able to get my first apartment in March 1998 by myself with my children. I survived Domestic Violence.

My Wins

- I heard the voice of God and was called to enter into the Ministry of the Gospel as an Evangelist in late 1997
- Completed Nursing Assistant Training and obtained a certificate and pin in March 1998
- Spoke out as a Survivor of Domestic Violence to a group of women from a church in the Spring of 2001
- Survived 2nd DV attack and divorce was final 2 months after the last attack
- Enrolled in school to pursue higher education and graduated from Erie Business Center with an AA Degree in Paralegal Studies in December 2002
- Completed my 1st manuscript for my story, which will be released this year
- I officially ordained as an Evangelist after 14 years of service in 2011
- I met a wonderful man and fell in love we were married November 21, 2015

- ✓ Kingdom Faith & Integrity International Ministries Inc was officially registered as a church in March 2016 and recently celebrated our 3rd year in ministry January 27, 2019
- ✓ No Domestic Violence Zone0 became official February 2017 and is registered with the state
- ✓ *No Domestic Violence Zone0 is currently preparing to go to its 2nd city in its 1st Tour: Beauty4Ashes2019

JILL ALLISON
Spinning Upside Down... Red Flags!

This has been the most tumultuous season of my entire half-century on this earth! Where do I begin? Let's start with the beginning of the spin-out!

So, 2018 was good to me! I became a new visual artist with a newly published website showcasing my work and as a result, began to build my business after many clients commissioned me to create original pieces for them! I also become a first-time author after penning a piece in an anthology along with 13 other winners entitled "Real Divas Win!" I was so pleased with what God was doing with my gifts that I started making plans for 2019 and I tagged it as my "net breaking year!" I was also doing well in my first career as a stylist and MUA of 30 years in the Chicago land area. Little did I know what was around the corner waiting for me would certainly "break my net" and flip my life upside down, literally!

2019 is here, I'm in a fabulous new promising relationship with major support, and as a result of a said new connection, my art business was elevated to a higher level by way of my amazing online store and blog created and purchased by my love interest! My art business began building even more and plans were made for me to visit Las Vegas to make new business connections! Life couldn't get any better for me!

The first few days in Vegas was a birthday celebration to which I enjoyed to the fullest! Day 3 and 4 felt a bit shaky, literally! Initially, I thought I had a little too much wine and that maybe hanging out didn't agree with me. Although I'm not a big drinker and didn't have much to drink I initially just brushed off the feeling of nausea and just decided to rest and I'd be fine. One day of rest turned into two and so on! Along with feeling nauseous I also experienced some imbalance...Didn't think much of it at this point, just thought, more rest is needed!

Day 6 and 7 I found it difficult to get out of bed and when I did get up to eat or do daily tasks, I'd find myself bumping into walls. Once I'd sit or even lay down, the room would spin or I'd feel a tumbling, upside-down sensation. WHOA! Now I was beginning to get concerned. I shared my concerns with my guy who then took me to the ER.

After sharing my symptoms with the physician, he decided to run some tests and as a result informed me that I had vertigo! Vertigo is an inner ear imbalance that can be caused by a few things. The doctor wanted to admit me immediately due to the severity of my experience to find out the cause but because I wasn't a resident of Vegas, the doctor decided to medicate me enough in the coming days so that I'd be balanced enough to fly home and see my primary. The meds I was given made me feel MUCH WORSE so after a few days of not taking the meds and eating nutritious foods I felt well enough to fly home.

Chicago bound-

I land in Chicago and as the Vegas doctor informed me, I experienced the spinning and tumbling immediately upon landing. Thank God I had planned ahead with the airlines and a dear friend to help me make it through the airport and get me home. Upon entering my home, I literally couldn't do anything but lie down. I rested and slept off what I thought was jetlag and vertigo and when I woke up that evening was in a worse state of spinning with new symptoms. I had numbness in my face on one side and tingling in my fingers. That's it! Time to go to the ER!

After being admitted and spending 8 days in the hospital, the diagnosis was not only vertigo, but the core cause of vertigo seemed to point to Multiple sclerosis (MS)! Needless to say,

I was stunned and in disbelief! What was MS? How could I have MS? But I've never really been sick....or had I?

During the initial days, I spent in the hospital the doctors and I went over my history in detail. I was asked many questions about the symptoms that I had experienced over the years but chalked up to isolated incidents. Come to find out, I had been "off-balance" a very long time! There's a running joke among my friends that I'm super clumsy but I never fall. I even affectionately hold on to friends when we're out and about. That was a major red flag I ignored! I had experienced double vision and blurred vision through the years but due to my visual impairment that has basically been a staple, no one thought much of that either, especially me. Just wear your glasses, Jill! Another red flag! Being a stylist and working long hours with inadequate meals was just an occupational hazard for me so whenever I experienced lightheaded-ness, I chalked it up to needing sustenance. Another ignored red flag! Yet another occupational hazard, according to me, was sore muscles! That can be explained away by long grueling hours standing on my feet! After 30 years of standing on my feet, it became second nature to simply treat the muscle soreness and carry on. RED FLAG!

So, as it turns out, I had been "off-balance" for many years and this incident was the culmination of all of the symptoms being exacerbated at once! As the days would creep on, I would experience more symptoms, tender tummy, stiff/sore neck, collapsing, soreness through-out my body it became obvious that my life as I knew it was about to change!

Once I was released from the hospital, I began this frustrating journey for help! Anyone who knows me well knows that I am pretty independent and self-sufficient because throughout my life I've had to be! If you read the original "Real Divas Win" you know that I'm low on blood relatives because I'm adopted so I essentially rely on my friends as my family! To my utter shock, the ones I thought would jump into high gear and be there for me, were not! Some not so much as send a text or made direct contact to see how I was doing. In the state I was in THAT is pretty devastating! Talk about "net breaking!" What I thought was my "network" was literally broken! On top of THAT reality check, finding agencies to help me figure out my next moves was like finding a needle in a haystack! To understand the severity of my diagnosis, I live alone and physically am unable to do simple tasks like stand at the kitchen stove and boil a pot of water for food. How was I going to get through this? Who would help me?

If I know nothing, I know the power and favor of God on my life! God sent angel after angel by way of my friends to help me! Some of the helpers I didn't even know well! People sent food, money, personal items, made calls, researched agencies for me to help this new normal not devastate me!

I have worked all of my life since I was a teenager so to suddenly not be able to work at all and have no income was extremely hard to navigate! To suddenly be totally dependent upon people and outside sources was hard to wrap my mind around. At times you couldn't be sure who was available to do what so you're always in limbo when you're basically in the world alone.

The thing I learned and have consistently understood was Who my source was! God has never left nor forsook me in any state I found myself in. And I say the state I found myself in because although I may not have caused my medical diagnosis, I was completely complicit in creating the perfect storm for my tumultuous year! I ignored red flags as it related to health, life and relationships! I was always in a state of imbalance when it came to who I allowed in and out of my space. Vertigo works on the body because it tricks the body into believing that it's not right side up! There is an exercise you can do while experiencing the tumbling upside down or spinning like symptoms to shift your atmosphere and throw your body right side up and eventually stop the spinning. That exercise needed to be carried out in my day-to-day life as it relates to connections and relationships. I constantly ignored the exercise to shift my atmosphere into the right position. Instead, I adjusted to the storm and continued spinning. So, once I was in need of something to anchor me there was nothing there...but god!

Through this unfortunate diagnosis, God began to peel back the layers and allow me to see who and what I really had. God began to steady my atmosphere, slow the spinning and allow me to stand firm by faith! I have a long road ahead and I honestly don't know what to expect from day to day but the one thing I do expect each and every time I am blessed to open my eyes is that God will be there waiting to steady my world! It makes whoever is not there, once I open my eyes, insignificant.

The thing that physical therapy teaches with MS and the vertical exacerbation is to find a focal point and keep your eyes open! The tendency is to close your eyes and go dark but If you keep your eye on the prize, you'll quickly release yourself from the nauseousness of uncertainty and everything will become balanced again! For me the prize is Christ! Always has been and always will be my focal point! With him, I cannot lose and I will always win!

I have never been one to allow anything in or out of this earth to stop me and I don't intend to start now! My prayer is that someone who may be experiencing an Imbalance will recognize the red flags and not ignore them. My prayer is that this impacts the lives of the readers and encourages you to refocus on what's important. At the end of the day, no matter what you face it's always going to be about your perspective! You can decide to allow your circumstances to flip you upside down or you can find your focal point and win!

If you'd like to connect with minister Jill Allison for speaking engagements or panel discussions, send your email to jillallison1111@hotmail.com

For original art and to commission Jill visits jallisonart.com

To connect with Jill on all social media -jallisonart

SHERMIA TAYLOR
From Homeless to Blessed

I was twelve years old when my mom moved over 1,200 miles from Virginia to Texas because my dad and she decided to separate. My mom took my two brothers with her because my dad wouldn't allow her to take my sister and I with her and my sister and I were my dad's only biological children. I remember the devastation and anger towards my mom, and I promised myself then that I would never make my children feel this pain, I could never leave my children. All of this was racing through my head as I was on my way from Virginia to Texas to stay with my mom because I had no family or friends willing to allow me to crash at their house with my three children after separating from my husband. I had left my children in the care of my father until I could get on my feet again, and the guilt from my decision weighed heavy on me.

My children were young, but I had hope I would only be gone for a few months or at least a year. I never fathomed that it'd take nearly five years to get my children with me in Texas, and a few times I had nearly given up hope of ever having my children again until one day in September of 2015 and my dad called me to tell me he was giving my children back to me.

Over the years, I called my children every day, which turned into every week, which turned into every other week, which turned into at least twice a month due to time zone issues, forgetfulness or my dad not answering the phone when I called or his claims that the children were in the bath and he not calling back after they've finished whatever activity they were engaged in. My dad had taken my ex-husband and I to court to get custody of my children, and, in the beginning, I protested, but in the end, my ex-husband and my dad convinced me that it was the right choice. I reluctantly agreed and right after he received custody, my ex-husband and I had to pay child support.

My children were only five, four and two years old the day I took them to my dad's house that fateful day in 2011. I felt so guilty and heartbroken because they'd never been separated from me for an extended period of time, and I was close with all of my children. My youngest took it the hardest out of my children, and it crushed me every day I would come to visit them and it was time to leave them again. It was a tough decision, but I knew I faced homelessness and hard times, and I didn't want my children to endure that, so I chose what I thought was right.

I prayed every day for two years that I would get a job, win the lottery or inherit money from somewhere so I could have my children with me. I had denounced my faith when nothing happened. I was losing hope and the desire to keep living. I was to keep my dad's revelation a secret from the children until our "exchange date", but I was so excited that I spilled the beans to my two daughters close to the day I was supposed to fly up to Virginia and bring them back with me. Friday, December 18, 2015, was the date that we had decided that I was coming to get the children. When I arrived at Richmond International Airport, I met up with my children and eventually my dad had left.

Since my mom worked at the airport as a reservationist, she was able to put my children and myself on the flight standby list. Due to heavy traffic around the holidays, on Friday night we had to stay at the airport. I stayed up all night with my eldest child so I could keep an eye on my son and youngest daughter as they slept. Saturday night we had to stay overnight again due to heavy holiday traffic, but my dad along with his girlfriend had put us up in a hotel for the night. The next morning the children and I made it to the airport and was able to board a flight from Washington D.C. to Ohio to Texas. For the next week, we were loving each other's company and seemingly picked up where we had left off albeit we all we five years older than the last time we lived together.

My kids were now ten, eight and seven years old now, but I was determined to not allow the past five years to determine our relationship. Everything was going great, they still loved and respected me as their mother, and I never stopped loving them. We were staying with my mom when I arrived in Texas with the children, but in the blink of an eye, we were thrown into the very position I was so afraid of putting the children in the first place. My mom didn't approve of my boyfriend of two years, so when he came to her parking lot so he could meet the children, she was very upset. The day after Christmas in 2015 my boyfriend had taken the children on a shopping spree for Christmas.

When we arrived back at my mom's apartment, she had taken the Christmas ornaments and presents the children had made for me, but I didn't say anything. The next day, through a series of events, my mom kicked the kids and I out in the snow in the middle of the night. I called my boyfriend, and he picked the kids, our luggage and myself up and took us to an acquaintance apartment. We stayed there for a month until we were accused of stealing. The five of us walked down the street as we pushed a few grocery baskets filled with our belongings after being kicked out, but as we walked, I prayed.

I prayed for deliverance for the situation and the safety of my children. A few minutes later, a few good Samaritans spotted us and offered to put us up for the night in a hotel. As the children slept, I stayed awake, dreading the next day and the days to come. The next night, after the children got out of school, we walked to a restaurant so the children could do their homework and eat. That night we had to stay in an apartment complex laundry room overnight to sleep, and my son and youngest daughter had soiled themselves.

It was the end of January, but I knew better days were coming, so I tried to stay optimistic as we walked the children to school in their soiled clothes. We washed them up at school and changed their clothes. I had decided that that was going to be the last time we slept on the streets. I applied for TANF and had just discovered that I had received funds on my card. It was the day before my son's birthday, so I was so ecstatic that we would be able to celebrate his birthday off the streets.

I immediately got a hotel, a surprise for the children when they got out of school, and they rejoiced. We spent a week at the hotel until the first day of February, when I got a welcomed surprise. My son is autistic, so he receives SSI from the government. The first thing I did when I received the money was to buy a car. I found a car online for sale and it was only $600!

My boyfriend and I decided that a car would be the best investment with the money because on days we couldn't afford a hotel, we could at least have a place to sleep and we wouldn't have to lug all our belongings with us around town. I made the car a surprise and revealed the car to the children when I picked them up from school. As time went by, we slept in the car, went to a restaurant or store in the mornings so the children could wash up and get ready for school and then took the children to school. My boyfriend and I put in applications and went to job interviews while the children were at school. I had begun attending the Texas Workforce and applied for jobs per requirement for TANF, but I couldn't get any leads. When the children got out of school, we'd take the children to a restaurant or store so they could eat and complete their homework.

I prayed for change, but my hope was dwindling. One day, when the kids were doing their homework at a local Whole

Foods, a security officer for the establishment asked if we needed help. I told the security guard about our position, and the next day her supervisor called me and told me they were going to put us in a hotel for a week and sign us up for housing. Local government housing accommodated us in an extended stay hotel for three months and I received a housing voucher. For three months I searched for housing with the voucher that housing provided, but on our last day at the extended stay, I still hadn't found anything.

We were told to vacate the premises because the extended stay visit was up, although local housing had assured me, we had a few more days. I had to pull the kids out of school early to help pack everything in the car. That day should've been the happiest day that year, but before we left the extended stay, I took a pregnancy test and I found out I was pregnant. I was distraught and worried about my new child to come, but I tried to be strong for my children, despite their intuitiveness. For the next eight months, we lived in and out of our car and random hotels.

My boyfriend went to work for a few temp agencies in August, so everything was starting to go descent, although we still didn't have a place to call our own, the car broke down every other day, being in close quarters was starting to take a toll on me, and my daughters would bicker every three seconds. I kept telling myself that it could be worse, but it didn't help my bipolar disorder and anxiety any. The doctor had put me on Xanax and bedrest because my stress level was starting to affect my unborn child. In November, after getting several complaints from my children about the abuse my son was suffering from his teacher at school. I confronted the principal yet again, but his teacher got word of it and called child protective services on our family stating that she had concerns because we were homeless. After my son's teacher nearly attacking me at seven months pregnant, I pulled my children out of the school and enrolled them in a different school. My stress level went into hyperdrive.

After being investigated, the child protective service worker closed the case, but I was nearly eight months pregnant at that time, and my due date was just a month away, so the thought of how I was to have a baby and we still lived in the car had changed to maybe adoption isn't such a bad option. I toyed with the idea, but I felt extremely guilty due to the suffering my children and I experienced from our five-year separation. Depressive thoughts crept in, but I continued to pray for change.

It was now 2017, and nearly two weeks after his due date, my second son was born - my first c-section. The hospital was extremely nice and allowed my family to stay in the room so the kids wouldn't have to sleep in the lobby alone. The hospital also had spoken to the hospital caseworker and they set up a stay at a shelter for the night I left to go "home" with the baby. When we arrived at the shelter, I couldn't find my state I.D., so they denied us for the night because my boyfriend couldn't go in with the children. January was cold, and this was the very thing I dreaded - having to bring my baby "home" to living in a car.

I walked back to the car silently praying for a miracle when a lady walked up and explained how she had gotten a room for the night at the motel next door, but she didn't need it anymore and they wouldn't give her a refund. She went on to ask if we'd like the room for the night. My whole family was thankful and stayed the night in the motel. I couldn't help but thank the Almighty for his work, even though we had to go back to sleeping in the car in the days afterward, that little hope went a long way. A month later my boyfriend and I got married.

A mutual associate had just moved into a new apartment and we were optimistic about the residence because although it was a one-bedroom apartment, it'd be ours. Our prayers were answered, and after nearly two months of getting married, we had moved into our first apartment. Yes, it was six people living in a one-bedroom apartment, but our prayers had been answered! My New Year resolution was to get a place to stay and publish my first book. I accomplished both, and I can say it was nothing but God. I am now on my way to starting a publishing company, and I can't do anything but give thanks.

Thinking back about everything, it makes me think about the poem titled Footprints. When I was doubtful about our position and questioning our fate, prayer worked. Miracles will be granted, but you can't give God a time limit, he gives you a time best suited for you. So, if you ever think your prayers are falling on deaf ears, remember that, when you need it the most, He will show up and show out and give you more than you ever even dreamed of! Push through your pain, past and hurt because there is a silver lining at the end. I am a Real Diva Winning, and this is just the beginning.

YOLANDA IRVING

On my way to the doctor all I could think was I am not going to live. On this beautiful summer day, the sun was shining, and I can still remember the scent of summer. My life was changing right before my eyes. Just when you think you are out of the loop here comes something else. All I could think in my head was not sickness, not me. In my mind I knew this was not meant for me. The question in my head was, God is this what you called me to? Would all my dreams and goals have to be set aside to deal with this? What would truly become of the me he created?

Who am I? Let me introduce myself. I am Yolanda Irving, a beautiful queen, born in Elkhart, Indiana June 5th, 1967. My life from childhood has always been filled with love and joy. I was raised in the era when folks knew what love truly was and how to express it. Back when grandparents were grandparents and knew what it meant to instill good morals and principles in the younger generation. The number one thing was belief in God and Jesus Christ and knowing why he died for me. There was nothing that would deter me from this principle. I was introduced to God at an early age since my grandmother was an old church mother. My goal in life has always been to love and be loved. The enormous love and affection from my parents are all a child desperately wants at the end of the day. Unfortunately, I didn't get that from my parents which took a toll on how I started to view people. I was forced to gather the love and attention from my aunts,' uncles and cousins. It's crazy but even today my parents still have unresolved issues with their own lives but still attempted to run mine. Yolanda has her own life and challenges to overcome. I've always known God had so much more for me to do and to place me in a position to be a blessing and grow into what he created me to be.

One thing I've learned on my journey is that there is always a higher power stronger than you created to try and stop you from evolving into the person you are meant to be. That power for me was my family. Like most of us, those who should have been our protection and guidance were those who walked away or totally ignored who we were. What God showed me was that those who were called to protect you and didn't was simply because they had a glimpse of you. I learned in life many people will back off because they can see the greatness in you. Everyone cannot handle your greatness. Never did I think I could use that word to describe me. I was always the one who was looked over, used, and totally misunderstood. I clearly see now that I was born to be different.

On September 9th, 2015 I began experiencing extreme heavy bleeding. This was way beyond the average menstrual cycle bleeding. After following up with medical appointments and doctors I was diagnosed with Menorrhagia. Basically, this means menstrual periods with abnormally heavy or prolonged bleeding. Although heavy menstrual bleeding is a common concern, most women don't experience blood loss severe enough to be defined as menorrhagia. I was losing an extreme amount of blood indefinitely and I had no idea what was going on. Yes, I believed in God but have never had to trust him on this level. Truth be told I had no idea how to. This area of sickness is normally followed by major surgery eventually, commonly a hysterectomy or something similar. Well, that's what it boiled down to and I was scheduled for surgery. I understood medical assistance can very well be a part of healing to correct this mishap my body was going through and all this pain I was having. So, it was set. Surgery it is. I had surgery; however, I was in pain for 7 months without medication I was still losing blood so they wanted me to have a hysterectomy so I wouldn't bleed anymore. My sister and granddaughter said no it was a money game. They said the doctors knew I had awesome insurance. that's when my granddaughter stepped in and knew I was not strong more surgery. "I wasn't healed from the first one" were my granddaughters' exact words.

During this period, after the first surgery, things in my body were not improving and I was still losing blood. One day my granddaughter asks me if I had an extra bible, I said sure and gave her the bible. My granddaughter's brother said she is still having that pain Rakiyah get the Bible she said ok. I went to my room and got into my bed. She asked if she could read me some scriptures from the Bible and pray for me, I said sure. As she began to read, she said aren't u scheduled? For surgery, yes, she said ok I'm reading now I said I'm listening now. As she began to read the scriptures whatever u ask God for, he shall do so. She continued, you ask God for healing and you need to have faith and trust God 's word. My thoughts at that moment were OMG. I knew this was God speaking through her. See most folks got it twisted. God will use the very person you least expect to get through to you. She told me to call the doctor and cancel the surgery. I replied, ok. The Doctor's response was, Are u sure? I said yes, my 9-year-old granddaughter told me to cancel my appointment with u and trust God, have faith and believe in his word. I knew I could trust God for a healing, and I did. My body loss lots of potassium as and my levels were low. I requested to see a therapist. I went to see a therapist after my cancellation so I could work on rebuilding my muscles and my body because I'd lost so much weight. I started googling different foods to see what could help me get my strength back. The lack of magnesium caused me to have migraine headaches that were very difficult to deal with.

During this time my life and my body were on death row. I knew deep down inside I could trust God like I knew he was calling me to. I knew it was no mistake that my granddaughter said that prayer. God has an amazing way of getting my attention. This is why today I can write this chapter and say I am Healed. God healed me. I am thankful forever. Every breath I breathe is because God loved me enough to save my life. I know there is still work for me to do. My win is that I'm still living right now. I have all my limbs, I'm healthy and most of all I have a voice to share this story with you. Life does not come with instructions but if you are given life freely and the option to believe Jesus does exist, test him and watch your results.

Some of my lessons through my journey has shown me that it's not about people and what they think about me. I only need approval from God. I had to realize how uniquely he created me. Once you realize your DNA only fits you, it will all make sense. I'm thankful for the opportunity to enjoy the remainder of my life. I can travel, enjoy my children and grandchildren.

SHERRY CAROL BEAN
Any Love Will Do

For a long time, I cried and felt really stupid and swore I was done with drugs. It was time for a change. I began to get myself together. I obtained a nice job making good money, I lived on the Northside on the high end and things were looking better. Little did I know I was being watched by one of the biggest drug dealers on the Northside who just happened to be the same guy that threatened to do harm to me before. It was like he was waiting on an opportunity to lure me back into the vicious cycle. Because of my lifestyle and anger towards my family I didn't have a lot of dealings with them other than on the phone; so, I was pretty much on my own. One day I was walking and I was approached by one of his workers who said he wanted to see me. Without even thinking I went; after all I didn't owe him any money and I was working and wasn't getting high so I had nothing to fear. As soon as I got to the apartment, I heard all kinds of commotion coming from the inside and when someone finally opened the door. Here was this big dope dealer and his friends sitting around drinking and bagging up rock cocaine. He turned to me and said, "Yeah, I've been watching you, and you don't mess with nobody, you don't have a lot of company and you wear a uniform. Why don't you try this out for me" and handed me a bag with a bunch of cocaine in front of everyone? I said, "Man, don't give me that in front of everyone." He said, "Okay" and snuck it to me. Then he said, "I want to use your house and I will pay your rent." I replied, "No, I can't do that." He didn't push it, but he didn't have to. He knew it was all a matter of time before I would give in to him. From that bag of rock cocaine, the downward spiral began; within two to three months, I lost everything. I stopped going to work, started selling things and I began letting my house be used for a drug spot. I began walking the streets all times of the night, scheming and plotting on how to keep the high going. Eventually the drug dealer stopped being interested in me or my apartment. I had become just hype to him. However, others were interested; they were called the nickel and dimmers. They would hit a lick, come to my house and we'd smoke. The low-ball drug dealers would use my place to sleep, eat and have sex in. All they would have to do is give me a bag and from there I ended up losing my apartment and having to stay with some crack addicted people who turned the lights off every time the drugs left. Since I had no money and no income, I started selling myself to the highest bidder. Once again, I thank the Lord because he didn't allow me to turn into a killer or spend my life in jail for a drug-related crime. I went from being a $10.00

hooker to being a "whatever I could get in a hurry" hooker. Before I lost my apartment, I received a call from my aunt telling me she had cancer. I remember crying and her telling me she was going to be okay. I hung up on her and began breaking things in my house. People were there getting high and I told them what my aunt said so they gave me extra. I went to see my aunt the next day, she looked at me and told me she was fine; she also said I didn't look right I was darker than normal; (sin has color). I told her I was fine and not to worry about me. That was as nice as we had been to each other in a long time. Later, I came to find out that her cancer was more advanced than what she said and was spreading rapidly. By this time, I had lost everything and had nowhere to go so I went to my aunt's. I wasn't even there a day before the phone rang and it was a young lady, I used to deal with calling to tell my aunt that she needed to watch me because she thought I was getting high. I heard my aunt say, "So you think she's getting high?" Immediately I grabbed the phone and hung it up, telling my aunt that she was lying but my aunt believed it. I didn't want to argue with my aunt, especially after she told me stress would agitate her cancer. I turned off the bathwater I was running, walked out her door, slammed it behind me, and said I would never come back again. Imagine me having an attitude because she wouldn't believe my lies. I walked to a shelter and went in with my cocky arrogant self and stated that I was homeless and needed a place to stay. They allowed me to stay there for a night without question, but the next day the process began. I said all the right things, but my heart wasn't in it, this was a game for me. What almost knocked me off my feet was when I found out that the very first woman I'd ever slept with also in this shelter. I also found out that this wasn't just a shelter; it was also a drug treatment facility that required certain things of you; like going to twelve-step meetings and going into outpatient care. You had to be up by 5:30 am and dressed by 6 am, ready for the day. On the weekends you had to be out by 6 am and couldn't return until 6:00 pm. At 6:01 pm you were late and had to find somewhere else to go. I mimicked what I heard other people say and did what they said just to have a place to stay. Until one day a lady showed some interest in me and I was off to the races again. When she left the facility, I left the facility; I stayed with her and her mom who was also a crack user. It was only a matter of time before I began using crack again. This young lady also had another person interested in her and they would visit her while I was there. She was in the same shelter with us prior to our leaving and before it was over, we were all getting high together; even though we could not stand each other. This run was worse than the first because instead of selling myself for money, I sold myself for a bag or whatever they would give me. One day, I was waiting on a park bench for my so-called girlfriend to return with some drugs, she never did. I finally reached the trap door that led to hell. I woke up determined to go back to that shelter, and if I had to, I was prepared to beg for help. With no money, I walked from the south side of Chicago to the southwest side where the shelter was located. It took me 5 hours to get there, but once I did, I looked into the director's eyes and asked her to please allow me to come back. She looked me in mine and said yes. A year later, I found out that she told someone the reason she let me back in was that she could see I was ready. She saw I was broken and needed some real help. Let me pause here and say thank you, Ms. Karen Crumb for seeing what I missed. I know you have transitioned to a place called rest, but maybe one of your children or grandchildren will pick up this book. I want them to know what you did for a lost soul like me. Okay back to the journey. Lying on the shelter floor I asked God to take my life, saying I've burned every bridge I've ever crossed, and nobody wants me. My family disowned me or so I thought. I said," God I give up" and it was then I heard a voice say, "Now I can get you up." And He did. I wish I could tell you it was smooth sailing from then on. It wasn't. I stopped getting high, but the demons were still there, and I was still sleeping with women.

Low self-esteem was still there, self-hatred was still there, rejection was still there, abandonment was still there, loneliness was still there and so many others. Knowing that people have their own opinions about recovery and 12 step programs, I still need to say this, it was the 12-step program that started my journey with God. I'm not here to defend it because it needs no defense. I am saying it was there that I was instructed to seek God out and develop a working relationship with him. It was there that I finally felt as though I belonged and wasn't by myself. So, I have to thank God for instilling in the mind of man, something that can help save many lives one day at a time. Now back to the journey. Although I wasn't getting high, I was still struggling with the inner me. I was still the little girl that just wanted to run away and hide, the little girl who was still searching out love in all the wrong places, faces, and bedchambers. At about 9 months into my recovery my aunt died. I need to say this; before she died, she looked me in my eyes and told me she loved me. Those were the sweetest words I had ever heard come from her. I believe that was her gift to me and my gift to her was that I was drug-free. When my time with that particular shelter was done, I ended up moving back to the north side in a shelter that allowed me to work. I got a job at a car wash making decent money as a cashier, but every time I got paid,

I was taking the girl who left me in the park money to show her how great of a person I was and how she should choose me. Not only did she not choose me, but she also resumed getting high and once again I was alone. Now, I am not going to tell you about every relationship I had, that's not necessary, just know I had them. I suppressed my desire for men because I knew no one would want me. You see, even though my aunt transitioned, her words still rang in my head so much so that I began repeating them to myself. Anytime anyone would show any kind of interest in me I'd sabotage it either with my words or my actions, I found myself becoming the voice of my defeat. By the time I was 28 years old, so many spirits were living in me until I didn't even know who or what I was myself. All I knew was I wanted off the ride but didn't know how to leave the park. There was a constant war going on inside of me; one minute I'd be on an all-time high thinking I could do anything I set my mind to; then in the next minute I'd tell myself how stupid and worthless I was and how my aunt was right; I might as well give up on being anything more than what I was at that moment. Are you still with me? Good. Now listen, I'm only going to discuss a couple of more relationships I've had because they're relevant in my journey to redemption. But before I do that let me say this; I'm so grateful that God has allowed me to experience and live to tell about his saving grace and his never-ending mercy in the midst of a 12-year crack addiction and all that came with it. I say this because I know a lot of people who died in the horrors of their addiction never living out their destiny in the earth. I'm convinced this is why God has prompted me to be as graphic in my description of these things as I have. I was set up. The last woman to woman relationship I had was with someone who longed for love and to be loved just as I did. She has a beautiful heart and is a wonderful person and is now married to a man of God and is active in her church; God you get Glory! Before I say another word, I would like to openly apologize to her for the hurt I caused her naturally, spiritually and financially. You didn't deserve the hurt I caused you and for that I am sorry and hope that you can find it in your heart to forgive me. Some may be asking why you are saying that; well, it's because once you're in Christ you simply want to make things right where you know you were the one who created the wrong. In my selfish, self-centered state I hurt a lot of people who didn't deserve it and I refuse to act like it didn't happen. It happened all over the place. Okay, here we go. I was with this young lady Janet for 4 years, but I will only talk about the last year. Janet knew God and would tell me what we were doing was wrong. I didn't want to hear that even though every time she said it; something in me would agree with it. I know now it was the

Holy Spirit bearing witness to the truth. At this point I was working at a clothing store with a woman I couldn't stand. She was too holy for me and I was too big of a sinner for her. I heard enough of that God stuff at home and simply wasn't trying to hear it at the job, so all we did was say hi and bye. One day as me and Janet were walking down the street this same lady runs out of the nail salon, grabs me, hugs me and tells me the Lord is going to do some mighty things with you, I know because He kept me up all night long praying. She pointed that long nail at me and said you just watch. I was in total shock; remember we didn't like each other, and we didn't talk to each other.

There is so much more to my story. Grab the full book on Amazon. From Rejection To Redemption
One Woman's Journey
SHERRY CAROL BEAN

Real Divas Win ™ Volume #2

ALIADA DUNCAN

Only in darkness did I find my light, and only in rain did the sun wrap me in its warmth. Like many of us in this questionable existence of reality, I have had my fair share of agony. I have rumbled with the roughest and toughest of battles. Although pain pursued me endlessly, I will forever give God the glory. Because of Him and His infinite wisdom, I am carefully covered in every chapter of my life.

Misfortune began for me long ago, particularly in the womb. My mother was on crack cocaine until her third trimester with me. At the age of three, I was greeted with the warped stain in reality. I was prematurely initiated into the arena of abuse. Sexual exploitation greeted me like a judge handing down a life sentence to an innocent prisoner. Indeed, I was innocent, yet the perversion in a beloved family member decided to contaminate my waters with their pollution. Perhaps, they themselves were sexually abused, and this is the notion I chose to take on my road of forgiveness. Forgiving in itself would be something I would continually do in regard to those I love, in spite of their physical, mental and spiritual afflictions placed upon me.

Due to the sexual and physical abuse, I endured as a child, my introverted self-came into full form. As early as elementary school, I immediately became the shy, oddball amongst my peers. I remember graphically the feeling different than the other children. Undoubtedly, the chaotic experiences in the privacy of my home were to blame for my mental and emotional frame of mind during that time. Let me tell you about one night in particular that will forever stick with me. I was no more than six years old and my brother (who was ten at the time) was left home with the same family member who had sexually abused me. Well, this night was apparently not his night because he used any excuse to harm us. There was an issue with the toilet which he had caused damaged too, but in turn blamed my brother and I. He became enraged and began taking turns beating my brother and I. Even though I was the younger sister, I felt sorry for how my brother was being beaten and I spoke up for him, big mistake. My whooping became even worse than before. Then suddenly, he rushed us outside and told us to run. In case you didn't know, where we lived at the time was surrounded by dirt roads and swamps, so just imagine being forced to run through backwoods at night. Running was an issue for me because, at the time, I had issues with unexplainable pain in my legs. Nevertheless, we obliged to his demands and began running as he chased us in his car. My legs began to weaken and my brother, being only ten himself, had to pick me up and help me run. Reflecting back on that night absolutely reminds me of something out of a torture film. And to make matters worse, I was the daughter of two parents who exemplified polar opposites. My mother and father were literally like night and day. For example, my mom, who as a child suffered her own hardships through the school of hard knocks, grew into her own and decided to serve God. Not only did she build a business for herself as a beautician, but she also overcame the odds by going to wealth from welfare. My dad, on the other hand, being seven years younger than my mom, had a totally different outlook on life. He grew up in a two-parent home with a working father and stay-at-home mother. I often felt he suffered his own share of abuse as well, which possibly accounted for the harm he inflicted upon my mother. Not only was my father verbally abusive, but in certain fits of rage, he would become physically abusive as well. I watched my mother endure his antics along with his cheating. Even going as far as marrying the woman he cheated on my mother for years with. However, the times in their marriage served as a model for being unequally yoked with someone. My mom fought to keep her faith, God, while my dad adhered to the temptations of this world. Although I must say, the many nights I laid in bed, awakening to the sound of vulgar language and rampant rage due to their arguing, all the more encouraged my anxiety. Anxiety would become an eventual walking mirror, tagging along and making a nest in every area of my life.

By the age of thirteen, my parents decided to part ways and I decided to do my best to represent the masculine role in order to fill my father's shoes. This age was a special age for me, this was the age I realized I was spiritually gifted. My intuition only grew stronger as I got older. I experienced it all, from seeing dead relatives to healing my mother when she became ill. Dreams were something that was extremely prominent in my life. I would be warned about events that would later take place in reality. I recall how angles and prophets of old would visit me through visions, or how I would revisit different times in places which I assumed to be my past lives. Because of this, it only influenced me more to be there for my mother. I did what I could to protect her, even though through her own pain she resented me. According to her, I reminded her so much of her ex-husband. For instance, one night, my mother was working in her beauty salon, and the neighborhood we lived in was known for crime-related issues. Well, this particular night, she was finishing up a haircut on a client, and a bullet flew into her salon. The shot could not be heard, because the shooter had a silencer on the gun. As young as I was at the time, I made it my business to protect my mother. The salon was across from our trailer, but I told her to walk behind me, just in case the gunman came back. Now, with all that I had done to protect her, there was still unresolved hurt lingering within my mom, which caused her to unleash her poison onto me. The physical abuse I endured from her because of my parent's separation reinforced the mental trauma I had become too familiar with. Remembering the night, I was abruptly awakened out of my sleep, only to be staring down the barrel of a shotgun. One could only wonder why a parent would point a gun to their child's head, for absolutely no reason at all. I recollect that night so vividly because at the age of thirteen I had endured so much, I was not afraid to die that night, in a way I actually wanted to leave this world. There was a sense of mental and emotional tiredness that had overcome me. However, I realized my mother had her own bouts with heartbreak and bitterness that she was trying to maneuver through. I blame her for nothing, for we all fall short in the sight of God.

I was never one to believe in curses, however, by age fourteen I had encountered a lot. I was in a deep depression for the majority of my teen years. I had many questions about life and why I had to suffer so much. Again, during this period, it was just my mother and me, so we dealt with a lot together. Not all of our trouble was physical or emotional, but some were spiritual and paranormal. For example, my mom would often get sick and doctors weren't able to explain the reasons or cause for her ailments. Keep in mind that where I'm from, root working (witchcraft) is a second religion to the so-called Christians there. There are many tales and stories about how witchcraft caused the separation of families and caused death. Well, one day, in particular, my mother decided not to trust in God and head down to Charleston, South Carolina instead to see a fortune teller. We went there, and immediately it was apparent the fortune teller was a witch. The lady instructed us to go to a store and purchase a batch of bananas. My mom purchased the bananas and we brought it back to the witch. She ordered my mom and me both to select a banana and open it. Simultaneously we peeled our bananas and to our surprise, they both had this strange hairy black ball inside. The witch informed us that this meant we were cursed. During that moment I truly felt hopeless, but I guess that helped explained the problems that seemed to attach itself to our family. Little did I know back then, God was still in control of my destiny and no devil in hell could stop His plans for me. For the bulk of my life, my mom and I endured a lot together. I witnessed her long for my dad, hoping that one day he would come to his senses and rebuild their family because her vows before God were taken seriously. As I grew, and though never married, I understood the pain of waiting for something or someone that I could never have.

Being from the Low Country part of South Carolina, I witnessed a tremendous number of eventful moments. Whether it be incest, shootings, fights, abuse, witchcraft, jealousy, etc. I witnessed it all. This was more than enough motivation for my mom to make the huge decision of moving to Columbia, South Carolina. Now that I look back over my life, I realize that this was the best choice my mother made for us. I am convinced my life would be nowhere near where it is today if it wasn't for that big move in February of 2008. Yes, that was the year that opened a new chapter in my life. I was in the tenth grade and enrolled at White Knoll High School. It was definitely a culture shock for me because up until that point, I had never been in the presence of so many white people. It was a new world for me. I was also introduced to homelessness for the first time. My mother and I left everything we had and abruptly moved without a plan; therefore, a shelter was all we could rely on at the moment. However, with God's help, we didn't reside there long. My aunt informed my mother of a housing program, and while waiting for rental assistance approval, we landed an apartment. It was a small and cramped one-bedroom located by a junkyard. It was very cold in the winter and extremely hot during the summer. I remember the first night we stayed there in that place. There were no beds, so we slept on the cold floor. Roaches and spiders were everywhere. Thankfully she was approved for housing and was able to find us a nice three-bedroom apartment in a decent area. It was so refreshing to live in a nice place again. However, my troubles were far from over.

My mom was a woman of faith that was often tested through many different areas of her life. Whether it was mistakes with men, drugs, being a victim of satanic attacks, sickness, etcetera, she just always seemed to be a magnet for pain. Frequent visits to the hospital became the norm for us. Blood clots in the brain, lungs, and chest were enough to stress any child, but that wasn't even the bulk of it. She endured several heart attacks, car wrecks, and the irritation of repeated tumors growing her stomach. As her child, witnessing her go through this tested my faith in God. Although I often pondered His reasons for keeping her alive through everything, she'd been through.

With everything that life had presented to me, I still made a commitment to keep my sexual purity for marriage. I thought that if I didn't have anything else, at least I had my virginity. However, in life, things do not turn out the way you expect them to. While attending Midlands Technical College, I met my daughter's father. I made it my business to keep giving him the wrong number, but on one particular day, I decided to give him the right number. He was a very attractive guy, and something about him felt familiar. That familiarity came from a vision I had a year prior to meeting him. Therefore, when I met him in real life, I remembered he was the guy from the vision. However, this was also before I knew about "familiar spirits". Within a two-month time frame of knowing him, at the tender age of twenty-one, I made the fatal decision of giving him my purity. Silly as it may sounds, I did this because all of the signs pointed to him being my husband. Both of our dreams would mirror one another in regard to our future together as a family. We would be out together, we would have these weird encounters of strangers walking up to us saying things like, "You two are going to get married. In life, things happen, but you'll have to forgive him and he'll have to forgive you when you get married". So, with all of that, I foolishly thought that it was okay to sleep with him since all the signs were pointing to us being together anyway. I guess I forgot to remember the visions I had prior to getting pregnant that I would be a single mother. It is clear that we pay attention to what we want to pay attention to when it comes to love. That day I gave away myself changed my life forever. Not only was I introduced to STD's but was also introduced to a new level of pain.

With my child's dad, I thought I had finally found "the one." The visions I had of us walking down the aisle and reciting our vows of commitment wooed me stupidly. However, I had no idea that being in his life would destroy me mentally, physically, mentally and spiritually. I was always a woman in tune with her ethereal side, so I would have been better off listening to my intuition when I first met him. Nevertheless, I gave in to his advances and fell head over heels in love with someone who had no clue what real love was. It was obvious he had his own demons he was in constant battle with, and at the time I wasn't saved, but I knew God because as a child, my mother instilled that in me. However, knowing God wasn't enough to save me from being cheated on and verbally abused. It was bad enough I gave away my purity, but a year later I fell pregnant. I remember the humiliation I received from both him and his family. Disowning my child and asking for a DNA test. The DNA test was extremely bothersome because I knew he was the only guy I had ever been sexually involved with. I was alone the entire pregnancy. I was also sick the entire time I carried my child, which was probably a result of the stress. With everything I was going through, I was in college trying to retrieve my Associates Degree in Human Services. This was a time where my will and strength were tested because my mom also kicked me out. I was homeless, sleeping in the school parking lot or in my mother's driveway. I remember accurately, pregnant belly and all, the day I asked my child's dad if I could stay with him. He greeted me at the door and assuredly told me, "No. You know I'm in a relationship. I cannot let her go for you. Move back to the Low Country with your dad." He turned me away at the door with my little trash bags filled with clothes and tears welled in my eyes. Nevertheless, I remained a straight-A student and graduated with my degree regardless. The stress had taken its toll though because one evening I was in my room getting ready to take a shower, and I felt this stream of warm liquid run down my leg. Initially, I assumed my water broke, but when I looked down, it was a puddle of blood on the floor. I became erratic and afraid. By this time, my mom had let me move back in of course. She heard my screams and came around the corner and immediately called the ambulance. They lifted me up on the stretcher and hauled me off to the hospital where they performed an emergency C-Section. I was so heartbroken. Nothing was going as planned for my life. Not only was I no longer a virgin, but I was a single mom having a surgical operation just to give birth to my baby. This was more than heartbreaking, I always wanted to have a natural home birth, not get cut up on like I'm some experiment. The father of my child did show up at the hospital but did not stay long due to reasons with his girlfriend at the time. So, there we were, me and my newborn daughter alone in the hospital. That night I made promises to her that I am currently in the process of fulfilling, but even the nurse couldn't believe he had left us there alone by ourselves. That situation in itself should have been enough to awaken me to the pain I was choosing to indulge in, but it didn't. He would still come over and sleep with me, then leave abruptly to go be with his girlfriend. I was being used and I felt so helpless at that time because I was living in an illusion. It had gotten so bad that I had to fall on my knees one night and beg God to deliver me from the vicious cycle I was in. It didn't happen right then, but obviously He heard my cry because my life was about to change for the better. My life has changed, and I thank God for giving me strength to share and save the lives of others.

My Wins

An Associate Degree in Human Services (2016),

Bachelors in Social Work (2019),

Winner of Best Poet for "Poet Speaks Magazine" (2019),

Featured poet in the book "Stars In Our Hearts" (2012)

Amazon Best Seller (Several times)

My Books are available @ Amazon

Real Divas Win ™ Volume #2

CHERISE BROWN

The phone conversation that changed my life. I have decided to kick disappointments, blames and hookups in the wastebasket. Yes, I said it and it feels good to express myself. I realize that a life that is full of negative thoughts and shameful behavior will create fear and allow you to let people walk all over you. Why did you do it, Cherise? This is what I would often ask myself throughout my life. What I came up with was that I simply wanted others to be happy even at the cost of my being miserable. I would be so miserable if people would get upset with me. It began with my childhood, at age 8 as a young girl growing up in Chicago on the Westside. My mother and father raised me to always do what is right and look after my younger siblings since I was the oldest girl. I took on the mothering role which was a lot of responsibility for an 8-year-old. I didn't get a chance to grow up and play outside like other children. My shyness grew worse and as I got older and started to get my teenage looks. Then there was the name-calling from family members and classmates from the acne on my face. "Oh Cherise, your nose is big", and other things they would say. There came a time when I didn't even want to leave the house because I hated school so much. I never felt smart, so at the age of 15, I just wanted to sleep for days and not go to school. I attempted suicide and took 10 pills that night and nothing happened. I still woke up the next day and I couldn't believe it. I knew it was God that kept me. I slept well and attended school the next morning.

By age 18 my first son was born. I will never forget when my mother found out I was pregnant she was heartbroken. I had no plans set, but I remember the beating my mother gave me it was like the scene in the movie, The Women of Brewster's Place and it was terrible. I moved into my own apartment at age 23 having my second son. I left the church. I entered into relationships that were toxic always giving these men my all even risking my body in my heart.

God was still protecting me and I was the best mother I could be. I made a decision to no longer feel sorry for myself. I had decided to be celibate for ten years I felt so good in my body and my mind was clear,

I still was unhappy with some of my life choices. I kept holding on to my past the childhood abuse and bad relationship choices I made.

I would ask myself, why I wasn't married? I'm a good woman Lord and I waited is there something wrong with me. I raised my two son's and now there grown men. I'm still not married but I'm good with that. I have mastered the art of knowing you cannot buy people and the flesh is never going to be satisfied, trust God.

Now being able to accept who I am made me so happy finally I no longer look down, I look forward and move cautiously, I don't put myself down anymore. My nose is big and my smile is contagious my writing is uplifting.

Once I realized I didn't have to please everyone I really could begin to love myself.

I am encouraging and I'm now a real diva who is winning. In March 2018 I created a blog called, An Emotional Queen.

I have come to a point in my life I enjoy my company. Whenever you are feeling down pray because God loves you no matter what. We all get bad news throughout life. I thank God for healing me.

My greatest reward is that I never gave up. Keep trying to encourage yourself and be a blessing to others. You won't believe how good it feels to see people laugh and enjoy life. I thank the Lord for all the people he has placed in my path I could not do this writing without my sisters. Understand your purpose and use your God-given gifts. I dedicate this chapter to my loving family into my sweet grandgurl Lyric. I love you all so much.

LESLIE EPPS

I was once in a physically and mentally abusive relationship, I was singing with a rap group and that's when I met HIM. He had joined the group as a singer also. At first, things seemed great. My kids loved HIM (the whole relationship) because they had no clue and he treated them like king and queen. We would have weekly rehearsals and then immediately follow with cards and drinks. (I wish I had known what I was getting myself into). My kids loved HIM (the whole relationship) but that was the beginning of a four-year tragedy.

I had started to notice that he didn't want me talking too much when other people were around so he would cut me off while I was talking to people, I would get the "let me holla at you for a minute", the squinting stares from across the room, all with an intimidating smirk and a soft voice to appear that there was no anger. I got to the point where I would be so embarrassed that I would just get quiet. Not realizing the pattern, I was not paying attention too. He had not long after that started to drink heavily and would try and intimidate the other group members and would crack not so funny jokes on our friends. They would laugh and try to assure me that they were ok, but I could tell from their faces that they didn't care for what was happening at all. After they left that night, all hell broke loose, and I woke up with my first black eye. It didn't take long for them to stop coming around either. My life was changing directions and I wasn't paying attention.

Because everyone had vanished, I had started to spend a lot of time around his family. I loved his mother; she is one of the sweetest women I have ever met. Some of the family I could tell loved me, some just liked me, and others only acted as they did. I could tell that one family member, in particular, had no respect for me. She would say things to hurt my feelings all the time and I would not say too much because HE would defend his family. She told me that I was old fashioned, I didn't know how to dress and that I needed to go and be around my own mama. (I wish I was who I am now) I let it make me feel worse than I already had been feeling. Some of his family would even ask me why I was with him. I gave the dumbest answers. "He doesn't hit me all of the time it only has happened two or three times this year." "He only does it when he drinks too much". He has never done it in front of my kids, and they love him. I went from black eyes to bad scars, verbal abuse, furniture being dropped on me while I was pregnant and losing the baby the next day. I promise sometimes I thought there was a demon inside of him because

I swore, I heard two voices coming out of him sometimes. I hated seeing happy couples, I was jealous when any female was around, and he was nice to her. I felt I should have been getting that attention. He also was hardly ever home and at the time I didn't realize that was a blessing.

My last straw was when I got woke up at 3 a.m. to someone attacking me in my sleep. The lights were off and I figured out it was him. After I am confused and forced to wake up cause I was punched in my face so dam hard and I recognized his voice asking, "who did you just let out of the back door". I was sweating and trying to get out of that room. Finally, I got out and ran in the bathroom locking myself in. When I looked in the mirror, I found out that the sweat was blood. The whole right side of my face was swollen from my hairline to my chin. I went to work the next morning and said I was in a car accident. Guess what ya'll, that old faithful bus driver friend from REAL DIVAS WIN 1 (I had just met her at the time) she looked at me and said, "accident hell". She knew HIM very well and she witnessed HIM in action before. She stood by me and kept me encouraged until I got strong enough to leave. I really thank GOD for putting her in my life and we will remain forever friends.

It didn't take me long to start realizing that I needed to start loving myself and never accept being abused ever again. I also wondered what happened in my life that made me accept that in the first place. It was from me never feeling like I fit in anywhere, I got teased and bullied so bad when I first moved to Gary I felt like the ugly duckling I was upset because I felt like I didn't have the material things everyone else had, I felt like I was just not loved and that's all I was searching for. That's when I started to learn. Now I'm Winning.

FELECIA BELL

Wait, hold up 4th stage cervical cancer!!!!! What the hell. This was what I did not know would send my life in a whirlwind. I'm trying my best to keep my composure but, how can I? We grow up, make mistakes, learn from them, look to God for guidance and do our best, and then BOOM. That evil thing that snatched away your peace.

So, I guess you are wondering what all the talk is about. My daughter, I lost my daughter to HPV. Jesus help me as I tell this story. My daughter Shamika Walker contracted what is called HPV and did not know. Yep, that thing not many talk about, my daughter died from. You would think with so many cancer forums, support groups, and non-profits that there would be some education about this version of cancer. Well, I'm here to clear the air and start that conversation. There is not really any info about HPV, what it is, where it comes from and how it is linked to Cervical Cancer. My name is Felicia Bell, and this is my story.

That doctor visit, that was the moment turned my life upside down. From that day on, our lives were up in the air. My daughter just received a major announcement about her health, and it was almost like there was nothing we could do about it. My daughter was young. She didn't live the most perfect life, but then again who does. Scrambling and almost going crazy, we, of course, wanted to get a second, third and fourth opinion but kept running into a brick wall. They said she was in stage four of cervical cancer. It's crazy how you never hear much of these stories. The world supports breast cancer much greater so there is not much info available about HPV. You almost have to dig deep until you find what may look like a little bit of hope.

Shamika began to deteriorate right before our eyes. I couldn't think straight day to day praying and hoping for a miraculous healing like never before. Shamika had 5 children under the age of 18. This entire time it felt like someone had placed a huge weight right on my kitchen table and it could not be moved.

HPV is an unknown std/cancer you can contract through sex, oral and anal sex as well as through kissing. The symptoms can be silent but the but one major side effect is heavy bleeding, cramps, and an abnormal pap smear. Males can also carry HPV without knowing; this is something that doctors don't share, and this information is crucial. My daughter only had that little time, and we didn't know nor did the doctors know how to treat her and what was needed. My daughter (Shamika was really strong in all this I felt her pain. I had chills in my body. As a mother, you don't know what position you would play if your child had cancer.

God prepares you for things like this when you don't even know. All you know is to pray pray pray. Ladies, please take this info and go talk with the doctor and always take someone with you. Have your list of questions to ask. Women, we must have a good connection with ourselves and know our bodies from head to toe. My daughter always said to me mom, I'm bleeding really bad. I would respond and say, did you talk with the doctor and how long have you been bleeding? Her response was always for 6 months. This is not good people. Do your research and stay aware of what's going on.

Shamika was laid to rest on 12-4-17 and I'm still not settled in my spirit with how this all happened so fast. I questioned God several times. Finally, I met peace concerning everything and decided to fight with providing knowledge of Cervical Cancer. What causes it and how to prevent it from taking more lives. I would never want anyone to have to experience this. I found out cervical cancer is mainly caused by HPV which is rarely discussed in our community. I have studied and researched, and I decided to use Shamika's story as a testimony to help others. I created the Shamika Walker Foundation. Our mission and our goal at the Shamika Walker Foundation to inform the public and save lives globally through cancer prevention and early detection. Our vision is to Stop Cervical Cancer and HPV Before It Starts! MY GOAL IS TO BREAK THE SILENCE OF HPV + CERVICAL CANCER.

The Shamika Walker Foundation advocates and supports the prevention and early detection of cancer through Research, Education, Outreach and Advocacy.

We are based in Chicago but want our info to reach lives globally. Follow us on Facebook and Instagram under Shamika Walker Foundation.

www.shamikawalkerfoundationglobal.org

shamikawalkerfoundation@gmail.com

STAY TUNED FOR REAL DIVAS WIN #4

IN 2021

JOIN OUR EMAIL LIST AT

WWW.REALDIVASWIN.COM

TO JOIN OUR MOVEMENT

VISIT

WWW.REALDIVASWINANTHOLOGY.INFO

www.ingramcontent.com/pod-product-compliance
Lightning Source LLC
Chambersburg PA
CBHW071415070526
44578CB00003B/580